THE POWER OF
WE
DAY

MOVING THE WORLD
FROM ME TO WE

CRAIG AND MARC KIELBURGER

with a foreword by Mikhail Gorbachev

The Power of We Day
Moving the World from Me to We
Craig Kielburger and Marc Kielburger

Roxanne Joyal, co-CEO, Me to We
Dalal Al-Waheidi, Executive Director, We Day Global
Scott Baker, Executive Director, Free The Children
Russ McLeod, Chief Operations Director, Me to We

Shelley Page, Executive Editor
Katie Hewitt, Production Manager

Me to We
225 Carlton Street
Toronto ON
Canada M5A 2L2
metowe.com/books

Distributed by Greystone Books Ltd.

Cataloguing data available from Library and Archives Canada
ISBN: 978-1-927435-11-3 (cloth)
ISBN: 978-1-927435-12-0 (epdf)

Printed and bound in China by 1010 Printing International Limited
Text printed on acid-free paper

Me to We is committed to reducing the consumption of old-growth forests in the books it publishes. This book is one step toward that goal.

Book and cover design by Erin Aubrey

WHAT'S INSIDE
THE POWER OF WE DAY

WHAT'S INSIDE
THE POWER OF WE DAY

126

52

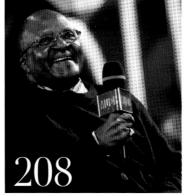
208

30

FOREWORD
BY MIKHAIL GORBACHEV

When I think of the many reasons why we must work across countries and continents for a better world, I think first of my great-granddaughter, Alexandra. At just five years old, she has her entire life ahead of her. I worry about what the future holds for her. Will she live in a world that is safe, just, and humane?

We Day makes me believe in the future. I have spoken at this impressive event more than once. Facing such a determined, motivated audience of young people fills me with hope.

For this reason, I agreed to write a foreword for the fine book you hold in your hands. It is a compilation of the many esteemed individuals and ordinary people who have appeared at this event. It is a valuable record of what Free The Children and We Day have accomplished.

We Day brings together young people working together on local and global causes. People, young and old, should know our collective history and learn from past mistakes and triumphs.

I inherited command over tens of thousands of nuclear warheads when I became leader of the Soviet Union in 1985. The United States held a similar number. Combined, we had enough blast power to destroy life on Earth.

My recollection is still crisp of my meeting with United States President Ronald Reagan in Geneva in 1985, where we declared "a nuclear war cannot be won and must never be fought." A year later, in Reykjavik, we agreed it was imperative to eliminate nuclear weapons. With leaders of other countries, we put an end to the Cold War.

However, in 2013, there are still many reasons for concern: Old threats to peace persist and new ones are emerging. The challenges of security, poverty and backwardness, and the global environmental crisis are as great as ever.

Young people have always been at the forefront of change. They would do well to understand these critical issues. We Day helps them understand and discover what issues are most critical to them.

And so I will tell you, there are many causes that remain important to me and are worthy of examination.

The environment must be our top priority today. In 1993, I founded Green Cross International, an organization whose main aim is to raise awareness of environmental issues and mobilize civil society for positive action. We need a dramatic change in our politics and our attitudes.

Access to clean water is an environmental, social, and health issue. As many as 800 million people have no access to safe drinking water, and 2.5 billion also lack basic sanitation services. A child dies every 20 seconds from water-related illness.

A project that is of particular importance to me is the Raisa Gorbachev Foundation, which I founded after my beloved wife died from leukemia in 1999. Its goal is to control cancer and leukemia among children, a growing problem throughout the world. We need to help those who suffer and to better understand why the youngest among us are increasingly being stricken.

Finally, I support new ways to empower young people, including the efforts of Free The Children. I urge young people to question leaders about what they are doing to address the main challenges that face the world today:

- What are you doing for the abolition of nuclear arms and for reduction of military spending?

- What are you doing to bridge the divide between wealth and poverty?

- What are you doing to save our planet from environmental disaster?

Some people ask me why, at age 81, I'm still working for global peace, still addressing young people like those at We Day. I believe it's possible to build a better world for Alexandra and children like her around the globe. We can do it together.

—MIKHAIL GORBACHEV, 2013

INTRODUCTION
BY MARC & CRAIG KIELBURGER

"I'm only one person, what difference can I make?"

It is a question asked by individuals, young and old, when confronted with the paralyzing self-doubt that comes with feeling small in the face of an immense challenge. Stacked up against the turmoil in our world, some feel lonely in their pursuit of good. How do they make a difference? Where do they begin?

We hope they'll find an answer in We Day.

We Day is a celebration and platform for millions of young people to learn about the most pressing social issues of our time.

Now held in Canada, the United States, and the United Kingdom, We Day celebrates student volunteers who've made a commitment to improve their communities—and the world. You can't buy a ticket to We Day: students earn their way in with service work in support of one local and one global cause.

It's both a spectacular show and a heartfelt gift to young people.

There are so many magical, unprecedented moments. Like when Grammy-winning songstress Angelique Kidjo appeared at the back of a packed arena in Vancouver to surprise retired Archbishop Desmond Tutu with her rendition of his favorite song. They ended up dancing together onstage. The Arch does a mean soft-shoe.

Or when generations collided with hip-hop icon MC Hammer and nine-year-old YouTube sensation Kid President doing the "Harlem Shake" onstage in Seattle. Key Arena was vibrating.

Sarah McLachlan sang "World on Fire"—a personal favorite of ours. Thousands of glowing phone screens swayed in the hands of her young fans as she sang. Jennifer Hudson made us weep with her soaring rendition of Leonard Cohen's "Hallelujah." It was a soundtrack for the stadium of volunteers, or as Hudson said, a room "filled with angels." When a new artist named Justin Bieber made a surprise appearance in Toronto, the screams that greeted him foreshowed his global domination of pop culture.

Beyond music, the We Day stage is alive with the hope and the promise of a better world.

We will never forget when Susan Mebet, a student from one of Free The Children's all-girls high schools in the Maasai Mara, flew to Toronto to thank singer Nelly Furtado for personally funding her boarding school scholarship.

Or when our good friend Spencer West, a double amputee, announced that he'd climbed to the top of Mount Kilimanjaro—on his hands.

Then there was the time His Holiness the Dalai Lama showed up early—he was so keen to speak!—and we raced to rearrange the entire event schedule so we could soak up his every word. We also can't forget when Sir Richard Branson surprised his daughter Holly onstage with a single red rose after her rousing speech.

For every incredible story from every world leader or renowned activist, there is a touching story from a quiet We Day hero: the young people who earn their entry.

Every year, We Day brings almost 160,000 young people and their supporters together from 4,000 schools. To earn their way in they participate in the year-long program, We Act, which provides classroom resources for schools and a support system for youth groups, individuals, families, and companies to turn inspiration into action.

We Day is truly the movement of our time. It means shifting focus from the solely self-centered "Me" to the greater good, "We:" protecting the environment, striving for equality, tackling bullying, apathy, poverty, and homelessness.

Every student has a place in this movement. Some kids paint rocks and sell them to support their local hospital. Others have led hundreds of their classmates on barefoot walks to raise awareness and funds for children without shoes in developing countries. Caleb Dawson, a student council president from Washington state, started a food drive that brought together 19 schools to collect more than 12,000 pounds of food. Canadian teen Mark Mannarn told the We Day crowd about Minor Hockey Fights Cancer, the charity he founded when he was 12, after losing his grandmother to pancreatic cancer the same year his mom was diagnosed with breast cancer. Mark's charity has so far raised $400,000.

The Power of We Day gathers words and images from more than 70 amazing people who have graced the We Day stage. It also features many of the everyday heroes who earn their entry. And it celebrates the We Day champions who support the cause and make it possible for students to participate in the event and year-long service learning program free-of-charge.

Our dream is that We Day will continue to spread to every corner of the planet: We Day Beijing. We Day Dubai. We Day Rio. We dream of the day when we all come together for the collective good. There's no future in isolation. What connects us is so much greater than our differences.

"When young people UNITE to take action they can create world change."

—CRAIG KIELBURGER

"WE DAY is a commitment to better our global community. We Day is the movement of our time."

—MARC KIELBURGER

—CRAIG KIELBURGER AND MARC KIELBURGER, SEPTEMBER, 2013

THE POWER OF WE DAY

MOVING THE WORLD FROM ME TO WE

THE BRANSONS
THE ADVENTURERS

Holly Branson once told us her dad, Sir Richard, will interrupt anything to take her phone calls. Once, she rang him after completing a crucial exam in medical school. They chatted for a good five minutes, dad peppering daughter for loads of details, her confiding her feelings of accomplishment—and relief. Once they'd caught up, dad casually remarked, "I better go. I'm standing onstage in front of 3,000 people giving a speech!"

Sir Richard was on a shark-diving expedition in some undisclosed Caribbean location when Craig called to let him know how excited we were to have Holly speak onstage at an upcoming We Day. Two days later, Sir Richard was out of his wetsuit and standing backstage waiting to surprise Holly, who'd never spoken to an audience of 18,000 people. Did we mention Sir Richard will interrupt anything for his daughter? He paced nervously on her behalf and when she was finished, dashed onstage with a single red rose in hand. Dropping to one knee, he told her how proud he was of her.

The Bransons clearly do things differently, whether it's business, philanthropy, or adventure.

A dyslexic high school dropout in the 1960s, Sir Richard is now one of the wealthiest Britons, best known as the founder and chairman of the Virgin Group's 400-and-some companies. He's an adventurer to the core, who meets challenges—speed sailing and hot air balloon races across the Atlantic—like the rest of us accept dinner invitations. He's also been called the "undisputed king" of the publicity stunt. He once bungee jumped off of a hotel rooftop to celebrate the inaugural Virgin American flight from San Francisco to Las Vegas. And he arrived in a spacesuit to the press conference announcing the launch of Virgin Galactic. He confessed to us he had to overcome his shyness to manage these stunts.

We got to know Sir Richard because he is also a devoted humanitarian. "Business has to be more than just a money-making machine," he told us. "If you can turn every single business in the world into a force for good then I think we can get on top of most of the problems that exist today."

Sir Richard has toured Free The Children projects around the world, and Virgin planes have run a coin-donation campaign to benefit our development work. Me to We Artisans jewelry and accessories are available inflight, with the proceeds going to support Free The Children.

But one of his greatest contributions—at least to us—was introducing Holly. When we met her, she had graduated from medical school and become a physician, but chose to work in a leadership role in the Virgin Group. She told us she felt she could do more good through business than by helping one patient at a time through medicine. She also told us she'd had a "very normal" upbringing despite Mick Jagger occasionally wandering through their house. Among the many hats

Holly wears, she works with Virgin Unite, the Virgin Group's charitable arm, to help determine how to harness its volunteer energy and spend its charitable dollars.

After traveling to our Adopt a Village communities in Kenya, Holly agreed to become the UK Patron for Free The Children. She told us the passion to do good is "in my genes."

"Every individual doing even the smallest thing can make a POSITIVE CHANGE in the world."

—HOLLY BRANSON

"If you're brought up with a conscience, then I'd think you'd feel guilty wasting the position you find yourself in. I'm incredibly FORTUNATE to be able to make a difference in other people's lives."

—SIR RICHARD BRANSON

NELLY FURTADO
THE SPIRIT INDESTRUCTIBLE

Nelly Furtado is more than your average triple threat. She's a chart-topping songstress in two languages, English and Spanish; a dedicated Free The Children Ambassador; and a fierce advocate for girls' education.

When we asked the Grammy Award-winning Furtado to travel with us to Kenya to visit Free The Children's development projects a few years back, we had no idea it would lead to an amazing friendship, designer T-shirts for our Me to We Style line, a new all-girls high school, and many other inspiring spin-offs. She chose the name for her 2012 album *Spirit Indestructible* from a line in our book *Me to We*. And she sold our Kenyan mama-made Water Rafiki Friend Chain on her concert tour, with each sale supplying clean water to one person for a year.

We're proud to call Furtado a close friend—and a household We Day name.

She's a kind-hearted soul who hasn't forgotten her roots. As a struggling artist, she worked as a chambermaid. Since making it big, she told us she always hides a big tip for those who clean her hotel rooms when she travels. Strong women—her mother and both grandmothers—raised her, and this has influenced the path she walks. "My mother, who I'd call a hero in my life, has a way of carrying herself with grace and poise and intelligence. She never reduced herself to a box or a category," Furtado recalled. "And she taught me that my opinion was just as important as anyone else's."

When Furtado was in Kenya she spent time with many strong mothers, and their daughters. She befriended a girl named Susan Mebet, who dreamed of being a doctor. Despite Susan's hunger for education, she didn't have financial support to attend Free The Children's Kisaruni Girls Secondary School. Furtado stepped forward with funds. When she visited Susan's mom to tell her that she'd pay the school fees, Monica burst into song, then ran out the door to tell her neighbors, who all came back singing. They encircled Furtado, who joyfully sang along.

"Many mothers are role models in their community and some of them remind me of how my mother inspired me when I was little," she recalled. She told us she'd never forget that moment. There have since been many others.

Furtado surprised the We Day crowd in 2011 by announcing she would donate up to $500,000 to support construction of a second all-girls high school in rural Kenya, to be called Oleleshwa. Furtado wanted to help the "thousands of Susans out there, with hopes and dreams but limited opportunities."

At that same We Day, Susan—all the way from Kenya—surprised Furtado onstage. It was magical to watch mentor reconnect with her inspiration. Many in the audience teared up, including us.

Furtado once told us that if she had a socially conscious superpower she would "make it so every person in the world could travel alone to the farthest corner from where they now live and live in another person's

shoes." She told us those people would come back enlightened by empathy and understanding.

She also shared with us what she hopes her legacy will be.

"I just want to make people feel emotions. That is why I am a songwriter. I believe that music is God's language and it's a bridge. It really brings people together. I believe in the rock and roll dream that can heal the world."

"I feel like LOVE is the issue of our time. Find that love, not just for your family or your friends, but also for that stranger."

—NELLY FURTADO

27

J.R. MARTINEZ
THE VETERAN

Private J.R. Martinez hit a roadside bomb less than a month into his tour of duty with the US Army's elite 101st Airborne Division in Iraq, in 2003. His Humvee was thrown, ejecting three other soldiers. Nineteen-year-old Martinez, trapped inside, was engulfed in flames. The skin on his face, arms, and hands burned away. Because he remained conscious, he can't forget watching his hands on fire.

It was more than a moment that changed everything for Jose Rene Martinez. It was the nearly three years he spent in recovery—undergoing more than 30 surgeries—that tested his attitude, changed his definition of service, and set the course for the rest of his life. After an especially grueling foot reconstruction surgery, his mother helped him learn to walk for the second time in his life.

The Brooke Army Medical Center in San Antonio, Texas, became his second home. There, Martinez was asked to speak to another burn patient, who'd just seen himself for the first time post-injury, and was struggling. Depression and body dissatisfaction are common psychological symptoms after burn reconstruction. Typically, patients become withdrawn, which makes Martinez's triumph over his disfigurement and pain all the more staggering. The nurses recognized Martinez as a positive influence and a potential role model. After Martinez met with the patient, the man opened his hospital room window to let the light in. He also opened his heart. And Martinez discovered he had a story that could lift spirits.

"Coming from the military, it's all about service," he told us. "I realized I could serve in a completely different capacity. Now it's sharing my story."

He's since told his story on the TV talk show circuit, and as a motivational speaker. In 2008, he secured a recurring role on the daytime drama *All My Children* and a stint on reality television; he and professional ballroom dancer Karina Smirnoff won season 13 of *Dancing with the Stars*. He's now an author and the host of a talk radio show for his local Los Angeles station.

Of everything he's accomplished, Martinez has humble hopes for what others might remember about his story. "I want people to know that I just believed in myself." Martinez is proof that no matter what life throws at you, your outlook is your choice.

> *"All it takes is one person to start a great MOVEMENT."*
>
> —J.R. MARTINEZ

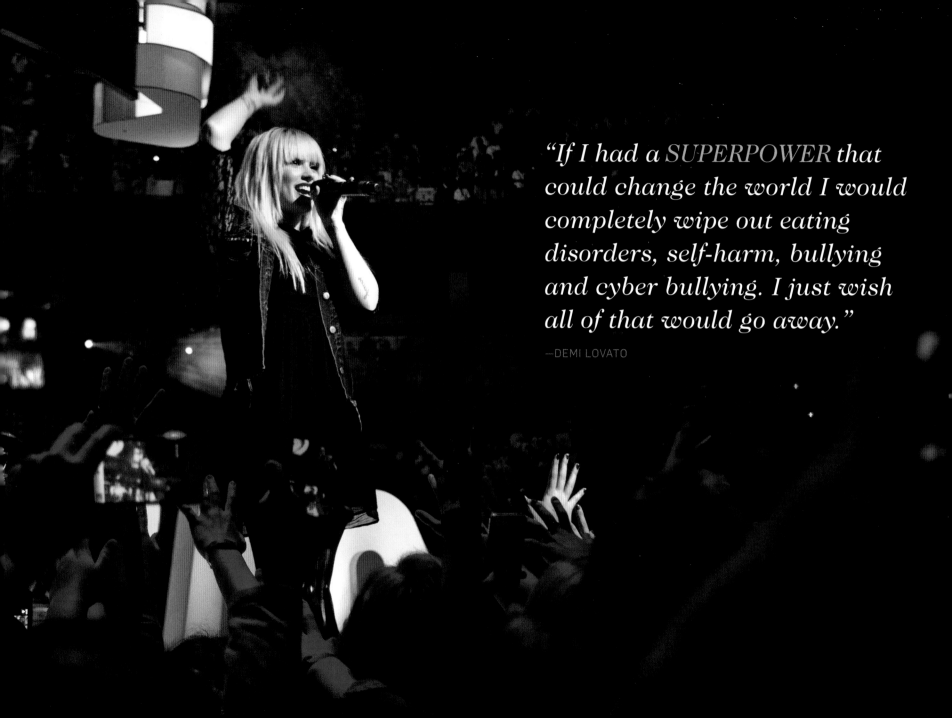

"*If I had a* SUPERPOWER *that could change the world I would completely wipe out eating disorders, self-harm, bullying and cyber bullying. I just wish all of that would go away.*"

—DEMI LOVATO

DEMI LOVATO
AFTER SCHOOL SPECIAL

Demi Lovato earned her first young fans at age ten playing with the famed purple dinosaur on *Barney & Friends*. Later she won more admirers as Mitchie Torres in *Camp Rock*. And she became everyone's best friend as Sonny Munroe in the Disney Channel sitcom, *Sonny With A Chance*. With three hit albums to her name, she is also a celebrated songstress.

But Demi Lovato is most admired for being herself.

She spoke openly about her struggles with an eating disorder, self-harm, and relentless bullying she endured when she was only 12. And in doing so, she has become a role model for millions of young girls wrestling with fragile identities and growing pains.

When we first met Lovato, she had the wisdom of a much older person, having been through so much. We were moved by her honesty and courage. She spoke to us of her passion to help others, especially those who have been bullied.

When Lovato first became an after-school television star and singer, schoolmates collected signatures on "hate petitions" against her, and held CD-bashing parties to destroy her music. A group of kids stood across the street from her house and denounced her. It made Lovato feel horrible.

Fortunately, Lovato received treatment and support, and made it through the "darkest period" of her life, "to the other side." She's determined to help others.

"Even before I was bullied, when I was seven years old, I knew that I had a purpose and there was a reason I was on this Earth," she told us. "I realized that everybody, no matter how little, or how old, you have a voice and you can do something with it, you can eventually change somebody's life or multiple lives."

When she talked about her struggles, she told us she hopes it helps others know that they can get through darkness into the light.

We'll never forget the reaction after she sang her hit, "Give Your Heart A Break," on the We Day stage. The young people in the arena fell silent. Some teenage girls wept, others looked like they might faint. All held their breath, waiting for their heroine to speak about her experiences.

Her message was powerful and direct, especially to those who were being bullied.

"This is something you can beat. This is something you can get through. This is something that won't bring you down."

Lovato is now an Ambassador for Free The Children, working with us to empower girls and spread her anti-bullying message across North America. We're thrilled she's on our team.

PETE CARROLL
THE COACH

We like to say that it takes a village to put on We Day. In Seattle, our inaugural We Day in the US, we needed Seattle Seahawks Head Coach Pete Carroll. He graciously agreed to co-chair the event while it was still largely unknown in Washington state, and spent the year leading up to it coaching for team We Day.

He taught us that it's not enough to win. "Always compete," is his philosophy for maximizing potential and pursuing our best selves, on and off the field. Which is why, earlier in his career coaching for the University of Southern California, he couldn't sit back and watch as students in Los Angeles inner-city schools joined gangs and fell victim to gun violence. Carroll spent late nights walking the streets to hear firsthand stories from gang members. In the city's notorious South Central district, he asked a 12-year-old boy what he wanted to be when he grew up. The boy shrugged, "I'll probably be in jail or dead."

These kinds of conversations spurred Carroll to create A Better LA, an organization that works to reduce gang violence by offering skills training and resources for people looking to get off the streets. A Better Seattle followed in 2011. It speaks to his genuine concern for the community that Carroll competed for kids that had largely been written off; some had given up on themselves. He wanted to give them something to believe in again.

"Kids are looking for purpose, but sometimes they turn in a negative direction," he explained. But he told us it's not enough to remove that negative influence, you have to give kids something to turn to. We Day is that something.

He addressed We Day Seattle like he might a locker room full of players. "Team We Day is 15,000 strong!" he roared. "The power to change the world is yours to own! But anything this great doesn't come easy. It's going to take great commitment. Vision. Dedication. Discipline."

Like all good coaches, Carroll helps his team realize they already have what it takes to win.

"I am so fired up and so PROUD to be a part of this great event dedicated to celebrating you!"

—PETE CARROLL

SPENCER WEST
POSSIBLE REDEFINED

Spencer West likes to joke that an amateur magician sawed him in half at a childhood birthday party and never put him back together. But the reality of his story, and all that he's accomplished, is even more incredible. A congenital spinal disorder rendered his legs useless. Doctors told West's parents that he'd never walk and that he'd never be a productive member of society. By the time he was five, he'd learned to maneuver on his hands; his legs, which he no longer needed, were amputated. Even as a child, with all odds against him, West pushed limits.

Twenty-two years later, in 2008 while on his first volunteer trip to Kenya to build a school with Free The Children, West spoke to a group of local school children about how he manages without legs. Afterward, a young Kenyan girl took to pushing West around in his wheelchair. She said, "I didn't know that something like this could happen to white people, too." She meant the loss of West's legs.

That moment gave him profound perspective and made him realize what his contribution to others could be. "I learned how simple it can be to give back by just telling a story," he told us.

West went on to become a Me to We motivational speaker and author of *Standing Tall: My Journey*. His story of determination and overcoming obstacles has since reached millions of people around the world. His biggest challenge—so far—was to climb Mount Kilimanjaro on his hands. In June of 2012, West summited Africa's tallest peak to raise money for clean water projects in Kenya. He climbed hand over hand, 19,340 feet, to give back to the community that changed his life.

Not long after the climb, Marc was driving with West through Kenya's Maasai Mara, when, wordlessly, Marc stopped the car and they both got out. They were searching for one particular patch amidst Kenya's vast grasslands—the exact spot where West met the little girl, four years earlier.

That search, and what it says about West, stays with Marc. After conquering Africa's tallest mountain, and the physical ordeal and media spotlight that came with it, West journeyed full circle to remember what had pushed him to the top.

When they finally found the spot, West said a quiet thanks.

We like to say that West is a giant. He's brought new energy and a renewed perspective to Free The Children. There is a perception among some that it's really difficult to change the world. But West, who has faced many challenges, proves that if he can do it, anyone can. He's redefined possible.

ON REDEFINING POSSIBLE

For seven grueling days, Spencer West fought fatigue, altitude sickness, and the extreme climate changes that come with climbing a mountain. On June 18, 2012, he reached the summit of Mount Kilimanjaro and raised more than half a million dollars for clean water projects in Kenya. We asked West what kept him going during his lowest moments on Africa's tallest peak.

"I've never been a quitter. The idea of giving up just isn't a part of my DNA. That and the whole point of the campaign was Redefine Possible, and if I can make it to the top then we can end bullying… we can change the world. We wanted this to be a symbol for people to recognize that nothing is impossible. And if you would just at least try, then something lovely can come out of it. I was making sure that I was that symbol."

SPENCER WEST

ROBBY NOVAK
KID PRESIDENT

He's pro-dance party. Sometimes he naps at his desk. His memos come in the form of paper airplanes and his office is made of cardboard. You could call him a fiscal conservative, but he probably wouldn't know what that is. He's Kid President, and he took office in 2012, at age nine.

Robby Novak was born with osteogenesis imperfecta, a congenital disorder that causes brittle bones. "It means I break easy," Robby said. His YouTube appearances as Kid President are a series of inspirational videos that encourage viewers to "make the world awesome." It was a family project started to share Robby's "resilience" with others. And it's an indoor activity, which helped him heal some of the 70-odd bone breaks he's had so far.

The YouTube series went viral, leading to celebrities appearing in his videos and a guest appearance by President Obama in February, 2013, via tin-can phone.

"What will you create to make the world awesome? Nothing if you keep sittin' there," Kid President prompts in his most popular address to the nation, with millions of views. Kid President: he's not in a party; he is the party.

PRESIDENT

ELIE WIESEL
THE SURVIVOR

Elie Wiesel lived the waking nightmare that saw six million Jews slaughtered in Nazi-occupied Europe during World War II. In 1944, at age 15, Wiesel and his family were deported from their village of Sighet, Romania, to Hitler's concentration camps. Wiesel watched his father slowly waste away, until he died of starvation and dysentery mere months before Allied forces freed the camp in 1945.

Wiesel held a silent vigil over his story for ten years. While studying at the Sorbonne in Paris, literary friends encouraged Wiesel to break the silence; they said his story should be shared for posterity. He said he had no words. Trying to ignore his experience was an attempt to lessen the trauma, he later told us. For years he held onto the belief, "that not thinking or talking about what took place meant that it didn't happen."

When words did manifest for his memoir, *Night*, in the late 1950s, they told of daily life at the camp, and of the destruction of Wiesel's humanity. His harrowing personal experience helped shape public memory, bringing the Holocaust experience into the collective consciousness.

When we first heard Wiesel's story, we were struck by his capacity for forgiveness. When we met him, he told us that he used his anger "as a catalyst to help and act, not hate."

As chairman of the United States Holocaust Memorial Council from 1980 to 1986, Wiesel preached the moral burden of remembering as an act to defy hatred. "Our remembering is an act of generosity," he wrote in 1979, "aimed at saving men and women from apathy to evil, if not from evil itself."

When Wiesel won the Nobel Peace Prize in 1986, the committee called him "a messenger to mankind." His message is one of peace and forgiveness, as he remains a tireless advocate for those who are silenced because of their race, religion, or nationality.

At We Day, he told the thousands of young people gathered that we are all responsible for one another, that our smiles and our despair are shared, that each of us is a gift, and that "indifference is not an option."

Elie Wiesel witnessed the worst atrocities of the 20th century, and still has an unshakable faith in humanity. He still believes in peace. He believes, "We are each other's hope."

ON LIFE

Indifference is not an option, just as racism is not, just as evil is not. The opposite of love is not hate, but indifference. That is also true of education. The opposite of knowledge is not ignorance, but indifference. The opposite of beauty is not ugliness, but indifference. The opposite of life is not death, but indifference to life and death.

What I had to overcome is to see in the other in the street, in the passerby, not an enemy but a fellow sojourner: not an enemy, but a friend, a companion, someone whose hand, when it is open, is a gift in itself. You will learn that nothing in the world justifies death. Remember: Life is sacred and therefore life cannot be replaced.

What I want to remain in you and with you is simply that whatever you will do in life, whatever endeavor you will undertake and whatever the road that destiny will take you, remember these few words: Always think higher and feel deeper. Think higher, meaning that simple things have their own beauty. Feel deeper, meaning feel deeper about one another. When I see a child, the sadness of that child darkens my universe. And the smile of that child gives me more hope than I can get from myself. But then this is the mystery of hope—it is like peace—the gifts that we give to another.

We are each other's hope. Thank you.

ELIE WIESEL, WE DAY 2009

MAGIC JOHNSON
THE SPOKESMAN

In 1991, Earvin "Magic" Johnson was at the top of his game. A long-time member of the Los Angeles Lakers, he'd won five NBA championships and three league MVP awards. One of the greatest players ever to grace the court, beloved by fans, Johnson seemed indestructible. So the world was blindsided when the basketball star revealed he was HIV positive—infected with a virus then thought to target "other people," like gay men and intravenous drug users.

We were just kids, but we remember this historic moment vividly. Our teachers showed us a television special where Johnson explained the nature of the disease and dispelled the myths surrounding it.

"Here I am saying that it can happen to anybody, even me, Magic Johnson," he said at a packed news conference at the Forum in Inglewood, California. "I just want to say that I'm going to miss playing, and I will now become a spokesman for the HIV virus."

He could have quietly retreated from the spotlight. Instead he fought both his own condition and public ignorance with the same determination he brought to the court.

Despite retiring before the start of the 1991-92 regular season, Johnson was selected by fans as a starter for the 1992 NBA All-Star Game. He played in spite of objections, including those from a handful of former teammates and other All-Stars, who feared they would contract HIV if Johnson suffered an open cut while on the court. In the face of controversy, he hit the game-winning shot.

Johnson now lives a remarkably active life, keeping his promise to be a spokesman for his disease. He founded the Magic Johnson Foundation to promote HIV/AIDS awareness and to create positive social change through community engagement and leadership. To prevent his HIV infection from progressing to AIDS, Johnson takes a daily combination of drugs.

We once asked Johnson where he gets his motivation. "I wanted to show that people living with HIV or any other disease could still get out there and live a productive life," he said.

He's a favorite at We Day for his candor, and for his bravery. He often tells students why he stood up to the bullies who didn't want him to play ball.

"Instead of getting upset, I decided to educate them, that you could play against a player with HIV and not worry about it," he said.

This extends to a message for young people to step in and defend all victims of bullying: "You win by making other people better. You can't be blessed until you bless somebody else. You can't be someone great until you do something great for someone else."

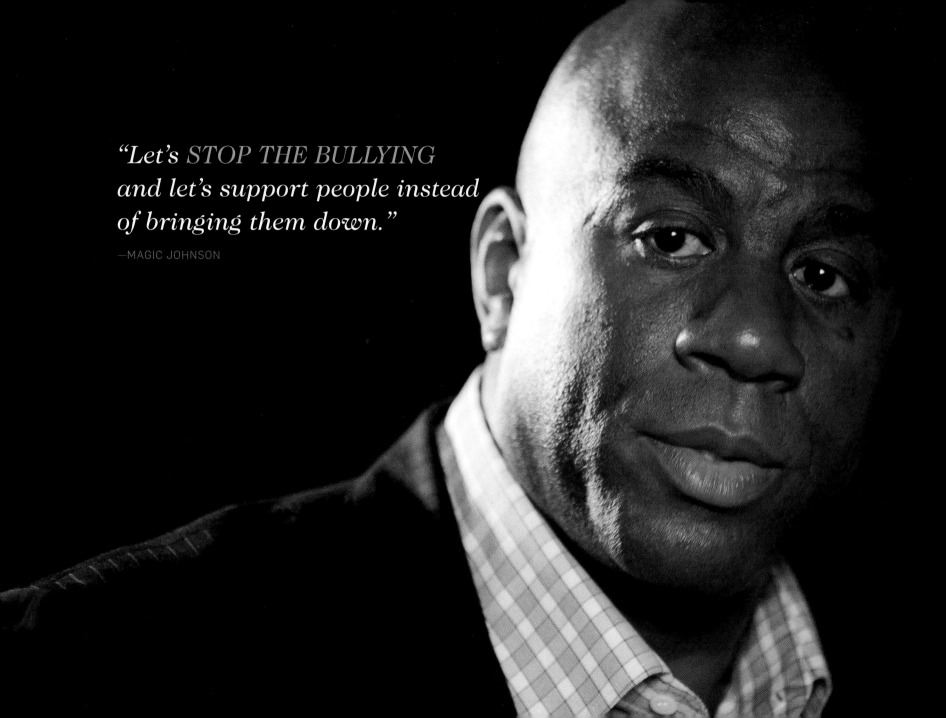

"*Let's STOP THE BULLYING and let's support people instead of bringing them down.*"

—MAGIC JOHNSON

LARRY KING
THE CURIOUS ONE

It is incredibly intimidating to ask questions of the man who has been called the "Muhammad Ali of the broadcast interview." Since 1957, Larry King has gone head-to-head with more than 50,000 people, including seven American presidents, Eleanor Roosevelt, Nelson Mandela, Martin Luther King Jr.—and Muhammad Ali, of course.

When we interviewed King on the We Day stage, the then-79-year-old sure knew how to connect with the young crowd—even though most were in elementary school (or in utero) when his self-titled show ruled CNN from 1985 to 2010. He got the crowd cheering by name dropping a few of the recent celebrities he'd interviewed, including Lady Gaga and the Jonas Brothers.

When we asked King what he has gleaned from all of the world changers he had interviewed, he coached the crowd on the art of listening. "I never learn anything when I am talking," he explained. And the art of curiosity. He is driven by knowing what motivates people; what makes them tick, he said. And he offered this advice: "Never give up when things look the bleakest. There will always be a tomorrow and when you look back, the biggest worries won't be that test on Monday, or the girl who didn't return your phone call, or that sad day your team lost. It will be better. But don't ever give up. If you want something, pursue it."

"If you're not CURIOUS, you're never going to learn."

—LARRY KING

MOLLY BURKE
A LIGHT IN THE DARKNESS

As Molly Burke went blind, her world shrunk. Light darkened, colors faded, and at her most vulnerable, her friends fell away. Teachers assigned helpers to walk her to class; some were embarrassed by her white cane. Burke became a target—she was bullied for going blind.

Diagnosed with retinitis pigmentosa in 1999 at age four, by 14 Burke had severe vision loss. The rare, degenerative retinal disease was killing off the light-sensing cells in her eyes. She began bumping into objects she could once see clearly. Near the end of eighth grade, she fell down the stairs and broke her ankle.

Her best friends were supposed to walk her to lunch, but one day eight girls led her into a wooded area behind the school, snatched her crutches and smashed them against a tree. They laughed, taunted her, then left her in the woods, disoriented and scared.

While coping with vision loss and relentless bullying, Burke struggled with depression, self-harm, and suicidal thoughts. At a time when most teenage girls imagine possibilities, Burke struggled with limits. "I was realizing, no, I might not be a brain surgeon and I might not fly an airplane," she told us. "I had to accept the loss of my sighted self."

The hardest part, she told us, was letting go of some of the activities she loved in order to spend time relearning how to perform basic tasks. Since age five, Burke had been a volunteer speaker for the Foundation Fighting Blindness but gave it up as a busy teenager with homework and other interests. Then one evening, her mother took her to a foundation dinner. One of the speakers gave a talk about overcoming obstacles and staying optimistic. And it hit Burke: "I realized my depression wasn't a loss of vision; it was a loss of hope." She'd also lost her fight, her drive and her passion. She decided to start speaking again.

Burke met Craig at an event and asked him about programs to help improve her public speaking skills. He handed her his business card and implored her to call him. A few months later, Burke moved from her suburban family home to Toronto to take a position with the Me to We speaking team.

It was a huge transition, a "life education," she told us. While she learned how to wash dishes, cook, and do all that comes with living on her own—well, almost, as her guide dog and "other half," Gypsy, is always at her side—she also gained what she calls, "a platform for the power of hope." She quickly became a role model for thousands of young people as her story touched We Day audiences across North America and around the world. As a Me to We motivational speaker, Burke recovered her passion and found her voice.

We're surprised when she tells us why she believes people respond to her story. "It's average," she says. "The fact that I lost my vision isn't average, but ultimately I'm talking about real-life problems. Bullying and mental illness. It's ordinary."

Burke is a face for anti-bullying awareness in North America at a time when high-profile teen suicides and cyberbullying have altered perspectives and playground taunts are no longer harmless rites of passage. It's now become acceptable, ordinary even, to broach the subject of bullying and stand up for solutions. She wants to say to those still suffering, "It does get better and you are not alone."

"I found my VOICE. And my voice is strong. You have your voices too and together our voices are strong, powerful, and loud. United, we are one voice."

—MOLLY BURKE

JEFF SKOLL
THE SOCIAL ENTREPRENEUR

As a kid, Jeff Skoll devoured historical novels that foreshadowed a world with too many people and not enough resources. He wondered, "But what can I do?"

At We Day, when Skoll addressed the generation that will inherit this dire picture, he said he'd felt powerless as a teenager. Many in the audience could probably relate.

Then Skoll explained what spurred him from meek observer to social activist. When he was 15, his dad came home with bad news. He had kidney cancer. While taking stock of his life, he told Skoll that he regretted spending so much time working, instead of traveling, living on a boat, seeing the world.

Skoll's dad beat cancer, and his words launched Skoll's resolve. He was determined to make a difference, to leave a legacy that would make his father proud. And as the first employee and first president of eBay, Skoll amassed the resources to tell stories that inspire people to get involved in the issues that face us all. In 2004, he started Participant Media, the production company behind thought-provoking documentaries and cinematic wake-up calls: *An Inconvenient Truth*; *The Kite Runner*; *Waiting For "Superman;"* *Food, Inc.*; *Good Night, and Good Luck*; *Charlie Wilson's War*; *Contagion*; *The Help*; *Lincoln*; and many others.

Participant Media is just one of Skoll's revolutionary social enterprises. His namesake foundation supports social entrepreneurs such as Grameen Bank founder Muhammad Yunus, and even our development work with Free The Children and our fledgling social enterprise, Me to We. We've gratefully relied on his wisdom and guidance for many years.

Skoll, the storyteller, believes we all have that potential to make a difference. "Your story is just now unfolding," he said at We Day. "Will you help eliminate poverty? Or will you cure malaria or AIDS? Or bring clean drinking water to everyone in the world?"

Jeff Skoll is one of our greatest unsung heroes, humbly carving a path that entertains, enlightens, and revolutionizes. As he puts it: "Only you can write your own story."

"What will your STORY be?"

—JEFF SKOLL

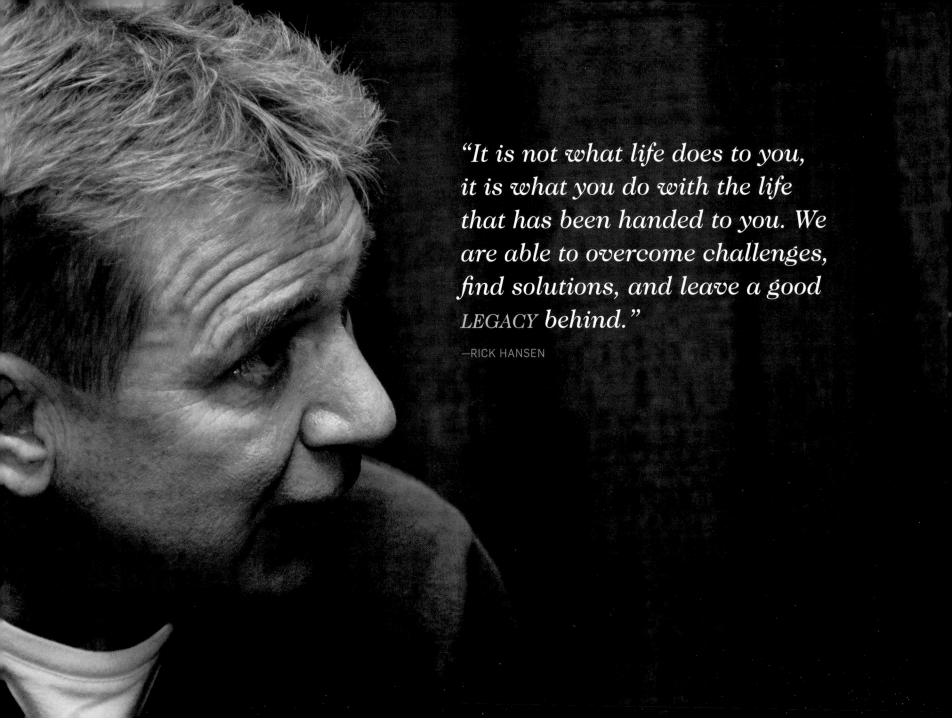

"*It is not what life does to you, it is what you do with the life that has been handed to you. We are able to overcome challenges, find solutions, and leave a good* LEGACY *behind.*"

—RICK HANSEN

RICK HANSEN
THE MAN IN MOTION

Rick Hansen is Craig's childhood hero, a wheelchair athlete who measured his accomplishments not just in the miles he covered—25,000 around the world—but also by the people he inspired. Hansen tackled every challenge with perseverance and quiet gratitude.

His youth reminds us of ours. "A whole world filled with the outdoors, fishing, camping, and being with family."

That world changed in 1973 when 15-year-old Hansen, returning home from a fishing trip, was riding in the bed of a pickup truck that lost control and rolled over. When he regained consciousness he couldn't feel his legs. The accident damaged his spine. "It was the most terrifying moment I could imagine." He would never walk again. Upon his return to high school, his gym teacher became his mentor. "I had a huge hill to climb," Hansen told us. "But he told me I didn't need my legs to be an athlete, teacher, or coach."

Hansen became a dedicated wheelchair basketball player, but found his strength in marathons. "It's amazing what happened when I focused," he said. He went on to win four world championship marathons and three gold medals at the 1980 and 1984 Paralympics. His world travels with the Canadian Paralympic team opened his eyes to the many obstacles the disabled face.

"I saw attitudinal and physical barriers for people with disabilities, so I combined my deep-seated desire to make a difference with my talent as a marathoner to hopefully change the world." In 1985, he formed an audacious plan: wheel around the world.

Two years, two months, and two days later, his Man In Motion World Tour had wheeled the circumference of the Earth through 34 countries—and raised $26 million for spinal cord injury research.

Hansen continues to inspire, passing the torch to the next cohort of world changers. At We Day Toronto 2011, he presented his Difference Maker medal to Me to We speaker Spencer West, who lost his legs at age five to a congenital spinal disorder. West was one of 7,000 difference makers Hansen selected to relay the medal across Canada on a tour to mark the 25th anniversary of Man in Motion. West took the medal even farther, to the summit of Mount Kilimanjaro on his climb for clean water.

Hansen tells us he wouldn't have changed the path he followed. Not for anything.

"Looking back on it, I'm one of the luckiest guys on the planet. I would never trade my life for the use of my legs."

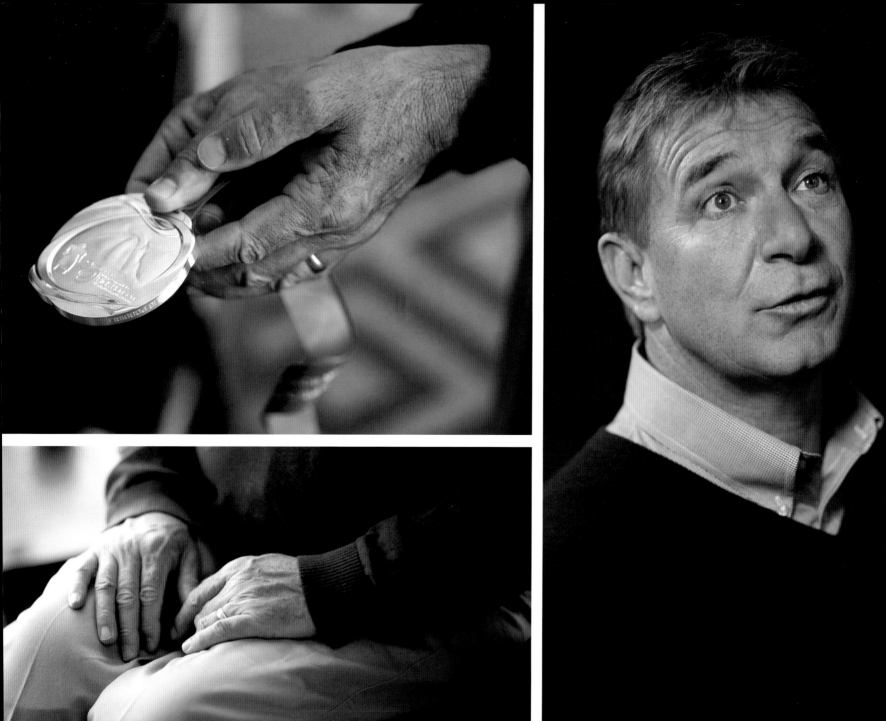

DEGRASSI
THE NEXT GENERATION

Far past the urban slums of Port-au-Prince in Haiti lies the rural community of Hinche, where these off-duty actors built a playground—the first in the province. In Ecuador, they helped build a rainwater purification system for an Indigenous community living in a remote, mountainous region of the Chimborazo province. In the Ghanaian fishing village of Asemkow, they helped lay the foundation for the community's first Free The Children school.

They are the cast of the Emmy-nominated teen drama *Degrassi*. Crossing the globe with Me to We Trips has become a rite of passage for the rotating cast that has featured Munro Chambers, Aislinn Paul, Drake (Aubrey Graham), and Nina Dobrev. The show's co-creator, Linda Schuyler, told us that a character's rawness comes from an emotionally mature actor. She wanted to steep the show's fictional world in real emotions—the compassion that comes with witnessing poverty and the empathy that comes from helping others.

The halls of Degrassi have seen their share of gritty teen drama. If those lockers could talk. Since the show's creation, the *Degrassi* series has followed the cast of characters as decades pass and classes graduate, tackling the most volatile social issues of each generation. Teen pregnancy, bullying, drugs in schools, and sexual identity were all fair game on *Degrassi* while they remained taboo in most other after-school specials.

Schuyler first approached us in 2007. As an advocate for Free The Children, she wanted to get the kids involved. And they are kids. These aren't 25-year-olds masquerading as teenagers on television. They're growing up along with the show, she told us. And they've seen We Day grow up, from cast appearances at the inaugural event in 2007, to co-hosting duties. They've weaved plots about fundraising for Free The Children into the show (with a guest appearance by Craig), and actor Raymond Ablack joined the Me to We speaking team to visit schools on breaks from filming. In a sense, we've all grown up together.

"We didn't go to Haiti to be there for the kids, but to be with them. And because we did, we came home INSPIRED, thankful for what we have, and ready to do more. Little by little, that's how we'll change the world."

—AISLINN PAUL

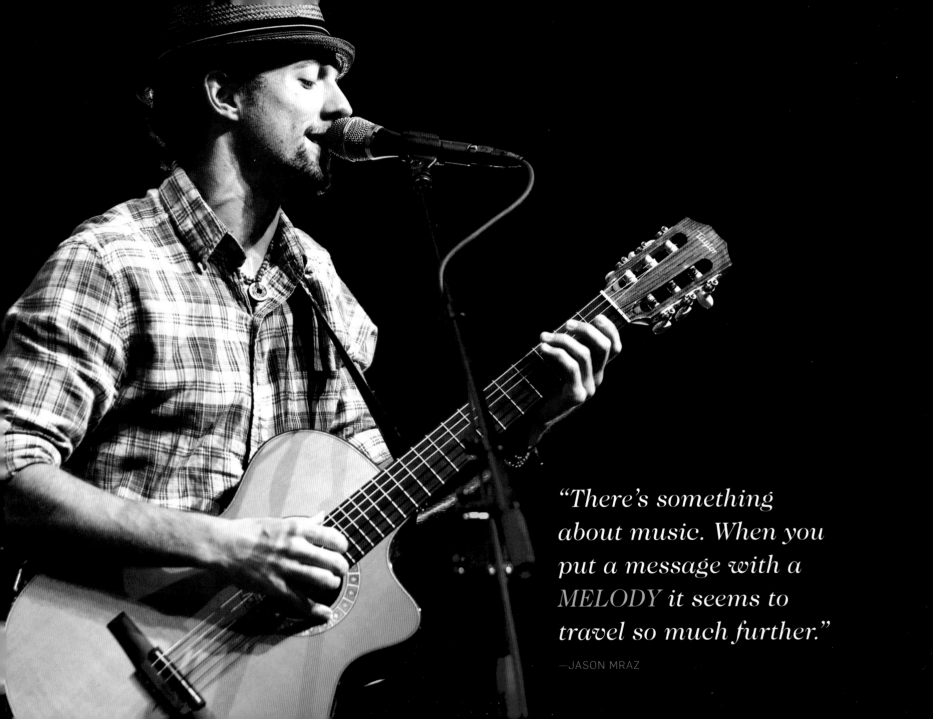

"There's something about music. When you put a message with a MELODY it seems to travel so much further."

—JASON MRAZ

JASON MRAZ
THE QUIET MUSICIAN

Sometimes silence speaks volumes. When famed musician Jason Mraz took part in our We are Silent campaign, he didn't sing a single verse; he didn't utter a single word all day. Mraz stood in silent solidarity with our youth members to raise awareness for the rights of child soldiers, child laborers, and children living in poverty who are silenced by exploitation. Mraz accomplished this feat while going through airport check-in and security on his way to a concert. That is true dedication to the cause.

The Grammy Award winner first became involved with Free The Children when he performed at We Day in 2009. Since then, Mraz juggles tour schedules in order to make additional appearances and support Free The Children campaigns. And he's always up for an adventure.

You might end up on a "trust walk" if you attend our Me to We Leadership Camp. Blindfolded participants must count on their peers' verbal directions—"Jump over that puddle. Left, no right!"—to guide them around obstacles on a short stroll.

The activity encourages teamwork and healthy risk taking in a safe environment. One summer, we wanted to reward a group for their service leadership at the camp. So we blindfolded all the young leaders and took them on an unusually long trust walk (that included a bus trip). When the blindfolds came off the group discovered they were in an otherwise empty arena. It had been reserved for a four-song performance by Mraz. The private concert highlighted the graciousness that Mraz, a willing accomplice, has exuded since we've known him.

SYLVIE FRÉCHETTE
THE UNSINKABLE SPIRIT

There are people in this world who have such a boundless inner energy that it seems the whole global energy deficit could be solved if only we could tap into their power reserves. Most inspiring are the ones who keep that positive energy in the face of setbacks and heartbreaks. Sylvie Fréchette is one of those people.

In the late 1980s and early 1990s, Montreal-born Fréchette was one of the world's rising stars in synchronized swimming, winning medals at international competitions for both her team and solo performances. She was considered a shoo-in for gold at the 1992 Barcelona Summer Olympics.

Then a week before she was to leave for Spain, Fréchette came home to find Sylvain Lake, her manager and fiancé, had committed suicide. In spite of the pain and loss, she headed for Barcelona where she delivered the performance of a lifetime. However misfortune followed her still; a mistake by an Olympic judge who pressed the wrong button robbed Fréchette of the gold medal. It took 16 months of fighting before the International Olympic Committee relented and gave her the medal she had earned.

Fréchette tells us she drew inspiration from the late Terry Fox, who attempted to run across Canada after losing his leg to cancer, to overcome the challenges she faced. "Just that image of Terry Fox, just running. I was like, 'Keep going, Sylvie, you can do it.'" Four years after Barcelona, Fréchette was back representing Canada at the Atlanta Olympics with the synchronized swimming team, who brought home silver.

Fréchette retired from competitive swimming, but has not rested on her laurels. She spent eight years as a performer and coach with the world-renowned Cirque du Soleil, and worked closely with high-performance athletes as a member of the Canadian Olympic Committee.

More inspiring, however, is her passion for giving back. Fréchette founded a school sports program that creates opportunities for children from all economic backgrounds to participate in activities like synchronized swimming.

Speaking at We Day, she challenged young people to think outside the box, to confront and to provoke, and to chase crazy ideas in order to create positive change.

"It takes beautiful, crazy people to make things happen!"

"It doesn't matter where you come from. What matters is how you feel and how you perceive yourself. When you're PROUD of yourself and you feel like you belong, you can do anything you want."

—SYLVIE FRÉCHETTE

SHAWN DESMAN
THE MOVES

We needed a We Day dance but we had some odd provisions: it had to be fun, easy for students and their teacher chaperones to learn, with moves compact enough to fit into cramped stadium-style seating (think upper body movement), and 18,000 kids had to do it simultaneously—without anyone getting an elbow in the eye.

So we asked singer, dancer, and choreographer Shawn Desman to lay down some moves to his track, "Night Like This." He's since had hundreds of thousands of kids out of their chairs and jumping on their feet at We Days across the continent. It's been done in classrooms, and at pajama parties. It's even inspired flash mobs.

In late 2011, we heard that 70 students at Grosvenor School in Winnipeg, Manitoba, were planning a We Day dance flash mob at a local shopping center. Instead of surprising the shoppers, they ended up getting a surprise. We alerted Desman, who showed up to dance with them. The look of shock on their faces was priceless.

Desman gets "goose bumps" when he sees a stadium full of people doing the dance.

"We're all in this together. We're in unison. We're in synch. We're here for one reason and that's to make change."

THE ANATOMY

OF THE WE DAY DANCE WITH DANNY AND TOUCH

STEP 1: CROSSOVER

STEP 2: THE BOOGIE

STEP 3: TRAFFIC CONTROL

STEP 4: SNAP-CLAP

EVA HALLER
THE CHAIRWOMAN

When teenage Craig first began traveling around the world to speak out about child labor, he'd often make house calls to potential supporters. He once hopped off a flight from Europe to be welcomed into the New York City apartment of noted philanthropist Eva Haller. She has led a fascinating and heroic life. She is a Holocaust survivor. She is also a great storyteller. But somehow, that first night, lulled by Haller's tales and sage advice, Craig fell asleep on her couch.

Craig can fall asleep anywhere, and that's perhaps why he survives traveling more than 300 days a year. But Haller has never let him live this catnap down.

Haller is the Chair of Free The Children's US Board of Directors, and a tireless supporter. As the We Day movement grows, she is chief among our many volunteers, an example to all who aspire to live a life of caring and contribution.

During the Holocaust, Haller's parents sold their furniture to buy flour and bake bread, doing everything they could to support the starving people fleeing the Nazis. Her older brother John joined the Hungarian resistance. Even though she was just 12 years old, Haller convinced him to let her tag along at night. They worked in a secret printing press, making anti-Hitler leaflets and then distributing them throughout Budapest.

When her city was occupied by German forces, and the Jews were being rounded up to be sent to a horrible fate, Haller faced off against a Nazi officer and convinced him she was far too young to die. Miraculously, he let her go, and she remained in hiding throughout World War II. John was killed crossing the Yugoslavian border—just months before Hungary was liberated.

When we asked Haller about the origins of her social conscience, she told us: "I remember the efforts of my family to keep others alive in Budapest during the war. I think especially of John. He was my true hero."

Haller made it to the US, where she cleaned houses by day and earned a Master of Social Work at night.

Years later, she helped pioneer the use of telemarketing in political campaigns and made her fortune in direct-mail marketing. She has been a philanthropist and activist ever since, serving many boards and causes, including our own.

She lives in Santa Barbara and New York City with her husband, Dr. Yoel Haller. They share their passion for philanthropy with their many grandchildren, some of whom are involved with Free The Children. We are grateful every day for her comfortable couch, and for her wisdom.

DANNY GLOVER
THE CITIZEN'S ARTIST

Renowned actor and social activist Danny Glover is a strong believer in remembering and respecting the past. The lessons we learn from life's interconnected journeys, he says, are not only valuable, but can at times offer unexpected twists. Glover, perhaps best known for his acting roles in *Witness*, *The Color Purple* and the *Lethal Weapon* franchise, inherited a strong work ethic from his social-activist parents.

For much of the 1970s he worked in community development in San Francisco—helping establish youth programs in the city's Mission District. The experience taught him that marginalized people need to participate in their own rescue in order to be transformed. He also read widely, notably a collection of speeches by imprisoned anti-apartheid icon Nelson Mandela, which deepened Glover's feelings of empathy toward others. "The story of South Africa is not only their story. It's all of ours."

Acting soon became a vital outlet for Glover. "As a citizen artist I realized there's value in what I do," he once told us. "It's the possibility of changing things." As an actor, he's continued to speak out for workers' rights and against racism, among many issues.

In 1987, Glover landed perhaps the ultimate part: the title role in the TV movie, *Mandela*, from which he gained not only an intimate understanding of one man's struggle, but also a new fan. Years later Glover met Mandela and the two became friends. The actor was awed and humbled to hear that the film was smuggled into prison for Mandela to watch in the waning days of his incarceration.

"I want young people to see that they are part of a much larger story—the human story. Every action, everything they do now translates into the POWER TO CHANGE themselves and society."

—DANNY GLOVER

DAVE WILLIAMS
THE DOWN-TO-EARTH ORBITER

Dr. Dave Williams comes across as an unlikely orbital adventurer. Of his teenage years he told us: "I was the one sitting *next* to the guy voted most likely to succeed."

Once you read Williams' resume, you'll wonder what the guy he sat beside accomplished in life. Williams has piloted jets, saved countless lives as an emergency-room physician, plunged to the depths of the sea as an aquanaut, and launched into space—twice—as an astronaut and neuroscientist, to name just a few of his out-of-this-world accomplishments.

Williams was selected by the Canadian Space Agency from 5,330 applicants for astronaut training. NASA also took notice. He was appointed Director of the Space and Life Sciences Directorate at the Johnson Space Center in Houston, making him the first non-American to hold a senior management position at NASA.

Williams served as an aquanaut aboard NASA's *Aquarius* underwater laboratory before being shot into space in 1998 aboard the space shuttle *Columbia* on a 16-day mission dedicated to neuroscience research. He led groundbreaking studies into microgravity and its effects on the brain and nervous system. Later, he took the shuttle *Endeavour* to the International Space Station, where he logged more than 11 million miles in space and made three spacewalks, setting a Canadian record.

Through it all, he remains humble. When we spoke with him, he shared one of his most memorable moments on Earth, which came just weeks before his first space mission.

Williams was at home one evening studying flight manuals when a neighbor came to ask if he knew CPR. An 18-year-old girl had collapsed on a nearby driveway after a severe asthmatic attack.

Without medical equipment, Williams resuscitated her until the ambulance arrived. Four days later, the girl came to visit. She thanked Williams for saving her life. He responded, "It's what I do. I'm a doctor."

But then he had a moment of clarity: "When you realize that you can intervene with just your bare hands and enable a person to survive, that's incredible. And whether it's saving a person's life, saving our planet, our community, or our children, it's the belief that yeah, we can all make a difference."

That's Dave Williams—the most down-to-earth guy ever to orbit the planet.

"It is important to LEARN from our mistakes and our setbacks, and not to think, 'I got it wrong' but instead to think: 'What can I do to get it right?'"

—DAVE WILLIAMS

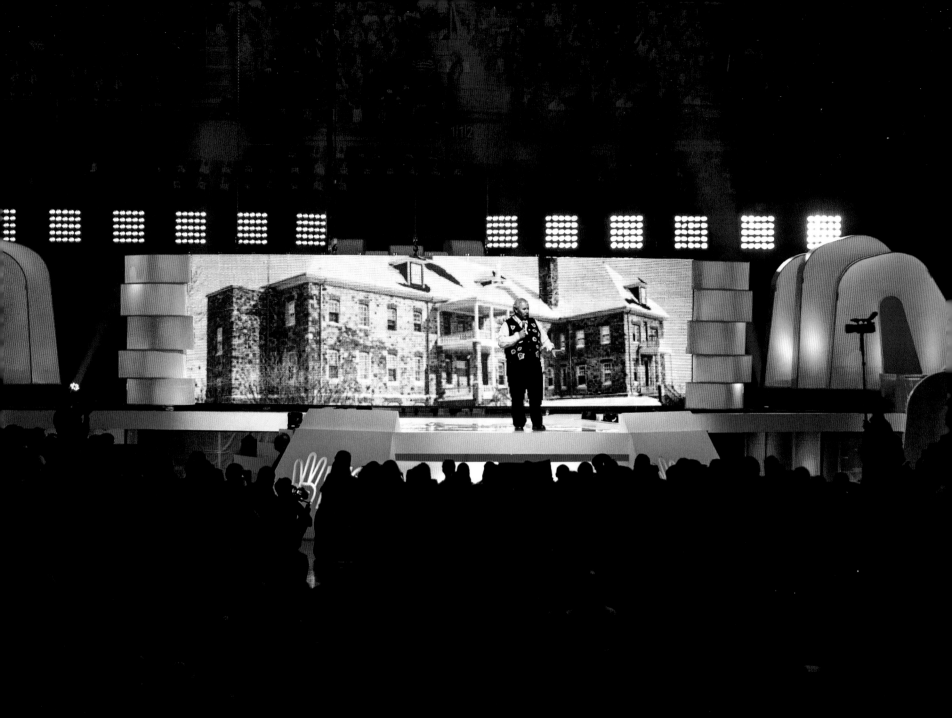

MURRAY SINCLAIR
THE JUDGE

The Honorable Justice Murray Sinclair carries stories of pain and loss for generations of Aboriginal children who were robbed of their families, language, identities, and futures. And he devotes his life to ensuring we all learn from these tragic tales.

Sinclair was born near Selkirk, Manitoba, on what used to be St. Peter's Reserve, and given the Ojibway name Mizhanay Gheezihk, which means "the one who speaks of pictures in the sky." He's always had high hopes for the future. His grandmother, who raised him after his mother died, helped turn his lofty ambitions into a calling. Her most important message to him: "You must take advantage of your opportunities and do something."

"I can still hear her voice today," he told us. "When I have those moments of weakness, when I think I'm going to stop doing my work, she'll say, 'No—you have to keep doing this.' She gave me a calling."

Sinclair became the first Aboriginal judge for the province of Manitoba, but he is best known for chairing the Truth and Reconciliation Commission of Canada. The Commission explores the legacy of Indian Residential Schools, where Aboriginal children were taken away from their parents and exposed, in many cases, to physical and sexual abuse. Sinclair told our young volunteers at We Day that these schools tried to "kill the Indian in the child."

"They caused a lot of damage to their identity, caused them to lose connection to their cultures and their languages, and that continued for seven generations—about 130 years. There are generations of survivors, and survivors of survivors, who have no sense of who they are or what their culture is or what their history is."

The Commission's mandate is to ensure that all Canadians know what happened in Indian Residential Schools, and to document the truth of survivors, families, and communities.

Justice Sinclair believes that Aboriginal students need an education consistent with their culture, sense of identity and hopes for the future, and that schools must teach respect between cultures and individuals. He implores the youth of today to demand the truth about how Aboriginals were treated—a sobering lesson for all of us.

"Talk to your schools about the fact that you want to understand the TRUE HISTORY of Aboriginal peoples in this country."

—MURRAY SINCLAIR

WILSON AND JACKSON
THE LAST MAASAI WARRIORS

Marc likes to counteract the long hours spent on airplanes and in boardrooms by hitting the gym. But in Kenya, the vast openness of the savannah beckons. No one is allowed to venture beyond the electric fence of Me to We's Bogani camp without the protection of a Maasai warrior—which is like the local version of a Navy SEAL. So Marc seeks the company of Wilson Meikuaya and Jackson Ntirkana—We Day speakers, authors, expert guides, and poisonous snake slayers. Marc puts on his $100 runners, while Meikuaya and Ntirkana tie on shoes made out of car tires, and strap on a conga, machete, and spear. The run turns into a jog, and then a walk, sometimes lasting for hours.

Marc seizes the opportunity to talk with Meikuaya and Ntirkana about their lives. Where we are each others' only siblings, Meikuaya has 42 brothers and sisters; Ntirkana has 21. Maasai families are made up of multiple wives and many half siblings. The warriors share what their family life is like and how they are adjusting to the changing roles of the Maasai warrior.

For generations uncounted, a Maasai boy's rites of passage included surviving alone in the wilderness and hunting and killing a lion. He would then become a warrior, charged with protecting and serving his community. Meikuaya and Ntirkana are the last generation of Maasai to complete this rite of passage—killing lions is now illegal in Kenya. Now the men—who think they are in their mid-20s, but aren't sure because the Maasai don't record birth dates—teach young boys that education is the new lion to be slain. To become a warrior, a high school diploma now replaces a lion skin as the trophy you bring home to prove you are ready to be a leader in your community.

For their part, Meikuaya and Ntirkana use these positions of influence to overturn hundreds of years of tradition by fighting gender norms to promote education for girls and end the practice of female circumcision among the Maasai. Both men have declared that when it comes time to marry, each will chose his own wife, who is not underage, has not been circumcised, and is educated. "We are telling young people to go to school, and that is how you can make a change in our community, in our country, and in the whole world," Meikuaya said.

When we thought Meikuaya and Ntirkana couldn't surprise us any more, they jumped on an airplane—they had to check their spears—to travel to North America to speak to schools, community groups, and thousands of people at We Day events across the continent. "We want to bring people to be like brothers and sisters, and also to know that we live in a small world together," said Ntirkana. Their message about what it takes to be a true warrior in the 21st century is as resonant for us as it is for the Maasai.

"With togetherness you have the STRENGTH to change the world."

—JACKSON NTIRKANA

"*HUMAN RIGHTS don't belong to any one side. They belong to all sides.*"

—MARY ROBINSON

MARY ROBINSON
TRUTH TO POWER

To say former Irish President Mary Robinson won't settle for the status quo is an understatement. She got an informal education in civil rights on the highly politicized campus of Harvard University, which she attended during the Vietnam War. She earned her Master of Laws there. Back home, the 25-year-old landed a job as the youngest professor of law at Trinity College in Dublin. She was elected senator that same year, in 1969, and became one of few women in a realm of "mostly old men," as she puts it. As a barrister in her late twenties, she sought out unpopular cases—the tenant taking on the landlord or the abused housewife seeking divorce. Even her personal life was controversial; a Catholic barrister, she married a Protestant lawyer, who became a political cartoonist.

When she was elected the country's first female president, she remained a divisive figure. Robinson told us that years after she'd won, a young woman approached her, shook her hand, and declared: "You were my first vote. And when I told my father, he nearly killed me."

When Robinson spoke at We Day, she said that social change sometimes means personal sacrifice. "I was a pariah," for backing controversial issues like legalized divorce, she explained. Her steadfast commitment to human rights went with her to office. She was the first head of state to visit both Somalia during the famine of 1992, and Rwanda after the country's genocide in 1994.

In 1997, Robinson became the United Nations High Commissioner for Human Rights. She visited Chechnya during the war and spoke to the Russian government about the conflict. In Colombia, South Africa, and Cambodia, she also spoke with human rights defenders and brought their messages to governments. "I spoke truth to power," she told us. "I wasn't being controversial for the sake of it."

We first met Robinson in 1998 at the awarding of the Roosevelt Freedom Medals. It was the 50th anniversary of the Universal Declaration of Human Rights, where she gave a rousing speech about the human rights challenges still facing our world. At We Day more than a decade later, we asked her about human rights challenges for the new millennium. She spoke of women's rights and maternal health, and about "climate justice" for her grandchildren.

"We may have millions of climate-displaced people. Water will be short. There may be wars over water. My grandchildren will live that. We need to see climate change as a justice issue. What kind of world will they inherit?"

"I have great faith that young people have an in-built IDEALISM."

—MARY ROBINSON

ONE REPUBLIC
THE GOOD LIFE

We met Drew Brown, Eddie Fisher, and Brent Kutzle in their dressing room at We Day. They're only three-fifths of the band One Republic (with Ryan Tedder and Zach Filkins), but it was still tough to keep up with the back-and-forth banter these guys have cultivated after ten years of touring together. They finish each other's sentences like siblings.

The pop-rock quintet from Denver, Colorado, has been together since 2002, or in the band's words, "since forever."

Their camaraderie has also cultivated a shared sense of social responsibility. All three mentioned the Golden Rule, but Drew summed it up best: "A system of giving what you would ideally like to get back is the best way to teach young people that there is a value in selflessness."

"It's important that kids see that even though they are not old enough to VOTE they can still affect change."

—DREW BROWN

PATCH ADAMS
THE BEST MEDICINE

The first time we met Dr. Hunter "Patch" Adams, he was wearing a dinner fork as an earring. It dangled from his ear as he proceeded to demonstrate his "disappearing trick"—hiking his oversized pants over his head and curling into a ball on the floor. Thanks in part to the namesake Hollywood movie that made him famous, many think of Adams as simply the clown doctor who heals through humor. In fact, he is a revolutionary with a vision of a world where love is taught in schools and compassionate, holistic health care is free for all. It's easy to dismiss him as off-the-wall, but he espouses a very humane idea of the world we should live in and the role we should play in making it happen. Adams is larger than life in every way.

"As soon as you find out what causes the problem, you have to say, 'I'm going to make my life a REVOLUTION and change these things.'"

—PATCH ADAMS

HANNAH TAYLOR
THE HOME BUILDER

We've always believed that children have a greater sense of the world than they usually get credit for. Hannah Taylor is living proof of that fact. At age five, Hannah was in her mother's car, driving through a back lane when she spotted a man digging through a dumpster. He was braced against the unforgiving chill of winter in search of his dinner. Her first glimpse of poverty through a frosted car window, and her life was changed forever. Hannah refused to do nothing about it.

She thought about the man every day. "My heart hurt," she told us.

In 2004, at age eight, Hannah founded The Ladybug Foundation, a charitable organization that raises funds and awareness to help Canada's homeless. She's since spoken to thousands of people around the world, authored a children's book, and had audience with Prime Ministers, statesmen, and corporate executives.

When she was just 11, Hannah's hometown of Winnipeg, Manitoba, opened an emergency shelter for the homeless and christened it Hannah's Place. Her small handprints remain outside in the cement.

Hannah is a We Day favorite, getting stadiums full of kids on their feet and lighting up Twitter after her speeches. It's no wonder. At We Day in 2012, Hannah had just turned 16, and she told the audience about fielding the constant question: What will you be when you grow up?

"I'm not entirely sure yet. But what I do know for sure is that the world needs us. It needs us to become lawyers, scientists, teachers, plumbers, writers, pilots, change makers. But what it needs us to do most is make our existence matter in the lives of others. Never stop caring."

When we chatted backstage, she told us she'd only just become old enough to "officially" volunteer (in her hometown age restrictions vary depending on volunteer placements). "Well, I was volunteering before now," she confessed. "I would go to a soup kitchen and sweep the floor—and even serve—so I think I was kind of breaking the rules." She said this mischievously, as if she'd really gotten away with something.

Hannah is our constant reminder that kids have an inherent idealism. More than that, they have the courage to act. Self-doubt isn't a factor unless it's imposed. We asked Hannah where she got the gumption to start a foundation at eight: "It came from me not knowing any better."

> *"AGE doesn't define what you can do."*
> —HANNAH TAYLOR

"One person can make a big DIFFERENCE, but together we can make a bigger difference."

—HANNAH TAYLOR

ON CARING

When I was eight, I started the Ladybug Foundation to help our country's homeless and hungry. But I need you all to understand that I am just a regular kid, who believes that together we can and will change the world for the better.

Working with people living in poverty, I've had the chance to learn many things, but I believe that the most important thing I've learned is the power of caring.

Don't be afraid of the hungry and homeless, be afraid of a society that doesn't care. Right now, hundreds of people are lining up at soup kitchens to eat. These are people. Human beings like you and me. We *need* to care and we *must* care. Caring is our power to change the world for the better! It's something that we all have the ability to do. Look around you. Every single person in this room cares. Every single one. How powerful is that?!

HANNAH TAYLOR, WE DAY 2012

DAVID ONLEY
THE HOST WITH THE MOST

When Marc was just 13 years old he concocted environmentally friendly cleaning supplies using his grandmother's recipes. Who knew that a boy, baking soda, and some elbow grease would garner so much attention? In 1992, Marc was awarded the Ontario Medal of Good Citizenship by the province's Lieutenant Governor—at the time, the youngest recipient in the history of this award. It was the first significant honor Marc received and he will never forget the formality of the occasion in the hallowed halls of the Lieutenant Governor's residence.

That's also why Marc still appreciates the significance, years later, of bringing hundreds of student leaders, active in their communities, to the official home of subsequent Lieutenant Governor of Ontario, the Honorable David Onley.

Since Onley first became a supporter of Free The Children he has hosted an annual event called An Evening of Champions that celebrates the students most active in the We Day program. Those invited are the young people who embody what it means to be a shameless idealist. In turn, Onley honors them for their efforts.

Onley is a model of kindness and hospitality, but he sets an example in so many other ways. At age three, he contracted polio, which resulted in partial paralysis of his legs and limited mobility; he usually gets around in an electric scooter. As a journalist and activist, he broke down many social barriers. During his 22 years at Citytv—a Toronto TV station—he became Canada's first senior newscaster with a visible disability. He has worked tirelessly to improve accessibility for all, in government and other public spaces.

He told us he wants to share the significant support he received from his family by extending that support to others, especially by helping them find meaningful employment. "People still believe the myths or misperceptions about hiring people with a disability, thinking if they look different or if they have a condition that has some degree of limitation it will be a problem," he told us. He hopes one of his legacies will be to break this stigma.

"If I had a magic wand, I would wave it to make people RESPECT one another."

—DAVID ONLEY

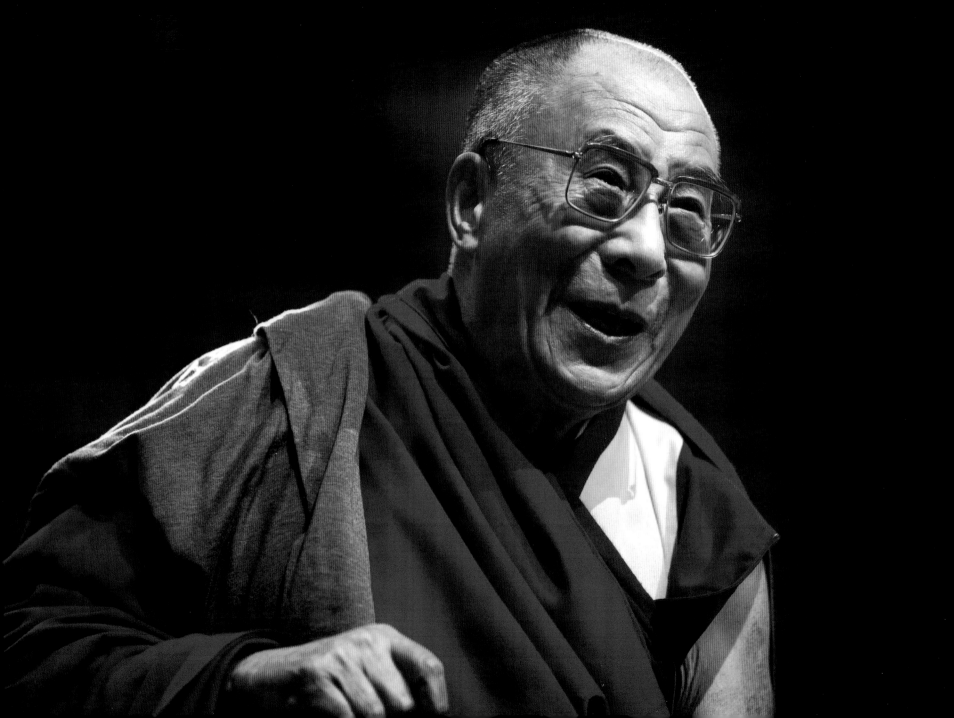

THE DALAI LAMA
THE COMPASSIONATE ONE

One of our favorite We Day moments was also one of our most frantic and improvised.

As one might imagine, His Holiness the Dalai Lama's schedule is always jam-packed. In 2009, he graciously agreed to appear at We Day, which landed on the final day of the Vancouver Peace Summit hosted by his very own Dalai Lama Center for Peace and Education. Knowing his time with us would be limited, we planned his timetable down to the last second, implemented extraordinary security measures to ensure his safety, and complied with every request from his entourage, including testing the firmness of the chair the Dalai Lama was to sit on while onstage. When the day arrived, we learned that the Dalai Lama was so excited to talk to the kids at We Day that, not only did he want more time, he was coming early! Protocol and our best laid plans were quickly abandoned. Improvisation was the order of the day.

The speaking time we had allotted for him suddenly quadrupled, shaving two songs off one singer's three-song set. As we scrambled to gather children to sit on either side of his chair, he also informed us that he'd prefer to speak directly to the audience in his broken English rather than through an interpreter as planned. Once onstage, instead of taking a seat in the specially selected chair, the Dalai Lama ambled forward to the very front edge of the stage. He instinctively wanted to be as close to his eager audience as possible, which achieved the desired impact, but sent several members of our We Day staff racing to the aisles directly below the stage to catch him in the event he took a tumble.

Of course in the end, it was worth it. We were all spellbound by the Dalai Lama's simple yet powerful message of peace, tolerance, and compassion. Despite the mad scramble beforehand, or maybe because of it, the Dalai Lama holds a special place in the hearts of the We Day family for delivering such a memorable moment.

His call to embrace inner harmony in order to achieve world peace has inspired millions around the world.

Free The Children was in its infancy when we first met the Dalai Lama. Together with a group of educators, thinkers, and cultural leaders we gathered in Stockholm to discuss the weighty question, "What is the greatest challenge facing our time?" Some suggested nuclear annihilation posed the greatest threat. Others argued that it was poverty, or the disparity between the rich and the poor, the Northern Hemisphere and the Southern Hemisphere. The Dalai Lama, worried for the future, said: "It is that we are raising a generation of passive bystanders." He argued that children today are afraid to stand up for what they believe in. This floored—and motivated—us. We took his words as both a warning and a challenge. How could we all do better? His words became our call to action. We Day, our signature youth empowerment event, is one response to the Dalai Lama's challenge.

"The time has come. We must make special effort to promote warm-heartedness and COMPASSION."

—THE DALAI LAMA

MC HAMMER
TOO LEGIT TO QUIT

At We Day Seattle, a 1990s hip-hop icon met a viral video sensation and the two riffed on an Internet meme—a pop culture mash-up for the ages.

When MC Hammer took the stage, he expressed gratitude to the young We Day crowd for their commitment to changing the world and encouraged them to shake the hands of their peers. Alone up there, Hammer needed a partner to shake with. YouTube star Robby Novak, better known as Kid President, bounded out to grab Hammer's hand.

Then the pair launched into the "Harlem Shake." The rap star and the pint-sized prez had the entire arena shaking, reminding us that we can have fun while making a difference.

Known for his distinct dance moves, impossibly baggy Hammer pants, and an infectious blend of pop and hip hop—think "U Can't Touch This" and "2 Legit 2 Quit"—Hammer balances catchy hooks with heartfelt calls to action. "I would never just do a bunch of songs and then not include something that would be about substance," he explained. Hammer also demonstrates his commitment to various causes by supporting organizations such as the Northern California Innocence Project, Literate Nation, and the fight against neglected tropical diseases.

NATE BERKUS
HEALING BY DESIGN

Oprah Winfrey reached out to us with a special request early in 2005. She wanted to build a school with Free The Children, which wasn't unusual as she'd been partnering with us for some time. But this school would be different; it would help Nate Berkus, her friend and *The Oprah Winfrey Show's* design guru, grieve a profound loss.

Berkus had been vacationing with his partner, Fernando Bengoechea, in Sri Lanka when an earthquake hit the Indian Ocean. The mega thrust of the sea floor caused huge waves, culminating in a devastating tsunami that hit several coastlines, including Sri Lanka's. Rushing waters left the couple clinging to debris, and to each other, until the current ripped Berkus' partner from his hands. He stayed afloat until he was found by strangers. A small group of survivors—one with a satellite phone—debated who to call for help. Berkus knew. Oprah cashed in every favor and contacted every private search and rescue team she could find. Bengoechea's body was never recovered.

Oprah asked us to build a school in Bengoechea's memory in the Ampara District of Sri Lanka, close to the very spot where Berkus last saw his partner. The school is now a vocational training center for young adults; one that teaches dressmaking, carpentry, motor repair, computer sciences, and other trade skills to the people of a fishing village whose coastline and equipment was largely destroyed in the tsunami. Built in part as a practical economic boost, the school remains a powerful symbol of revival.

Sometimes you meet people through tragedy. We accompanied Berkus to the school's opening ceremony in 2006, and we were humbled to be part of his healing process. The three of us were led through a procession of students to the plaque that marked the dedication to Bengoechea. All of us were in tears. The building, designed to withstand all forms of natural disaster, is meant to be a safe haven in crisis.

Berkus took comfort knowing that he'd helped rebuild a community. Those gathered at We Day Toronto in 2008 will also never forget the story of tragedy and rebuilding that he shared.

"The moment that you reach out to care for somebody, you're tapping into the ultimate GRACE."

—NATE BERKUS

ROBERT F. KENNEDY JR.
THE RIVERKEEPER

With his distinctive New England accent and Kennedy family charm, Robert F. Kennedy Jr. spoke at We Day about the importance of grassroots democracy in the fight to save the planet from environmental polluters—something he has been committed to since teaming up with Riverkeeper. The clean water watchdog began in 1966 when a group of concerned fishermen banded together to protect the Hudson River and the drinking water supply of New York City residents. As the Chief Prosecuting Attorney for Riverkeeper since 1984, Kennedy spearheaded landmark legal actions against large corporate water polluters. The Riverkeeper movement has spread across North America, protecting its rivers, lakes, and watersheds. Kennedy and the Hudson River fishermen are a shining example of the awesome power of We.

"The only thing that really works in a democracy is GRASSROOTS organizing, and with that we can change history."

—ROBERT F. KENNEDY JR.

HEDLEY
COOL TO CARE

Jacob Hoggard, Tommy Mac, Dave Rosin, and Chris Crippin have been a band for more than a decade, and have since become like any other family—loving and a bit dysfunctional. Lead singer Hoggard is well known for his unorthodox stage antics. As We Day regulars, they're often backstage pulling pranks on each other. They're the last to leave the after-party and the first to decide that an after-after-party is in order. So when the guys planned a Me to We Trip to Kenya in 2010, there were questions about additional travel insurance—only half jokingly.

Cultures collapsed when the band's tattooed limbs shook the hands of Maasai chiefs. But instead of clashing, the local chiefs were fascinated by the band's markings, which resembled the traditional burn designs that prove strength in Maasai culture. The stretched earlobes of guitarist Rosin matched the local customs and jewelry. The musicians were soon named honorary Maasai warriors.

We learned from each other. Hedley challenged the stereotypes about reckless rock stars, and their visits to our development projects overseas opened their eyes to "the realities of the world," Hoggard told us. "Free The Children has given me a sense of accountability." Before he got involved, he says he was "selfish with no real sense of responsibility for my community."

Hedley has rocked We Day's world in nearly every event city. We're proud to call them our official Ambassadors, and part of our own extended Free The Children family.

"During a volunteer trip to India with Free The Children, I met an elderly local man who asked about what we were doing in the country. When I described the work, he nodded his head and said: 'This is good.' He voiced a question that has forever stayed with me: 'Why do so many seek to create a better world for our children? We need to CREATE better children for our world.'"

—JACOB HOGGARD

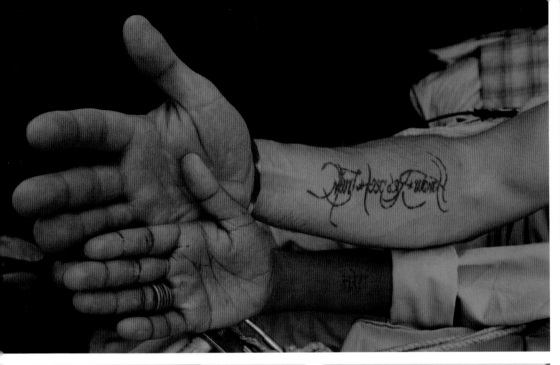

SHAWN ATLEO
THE CHIEF

Sometimes we're lucky enough to watch a historic moment unfold before our eyes.

In a tiny building out on the Kenyan savannah, we were privileged to listen in as Shawn Atleo, National Chief of the Assembly of First Nations and a hereditary chief of Ahousaht First Nation, sat down with a Maasai chief and discovered the common ideals and challenges that bring together cultures from worlds apart.

Language proved no barrier as the two chiefs shared the beauty of coming from a tribal people with deep links to the land. In that room that would soon become a new school for Maasai children, the men talked about the challenges of preserving traditional heritage in the face of outside influences and a changing world around them.

As the Maasai chief spoke of his people's fears about Western schooling, Atleo related the experiences of Canada's First Nations, who, for more than a hundred years, were taken from their homes and families, their culture and language suppressed in residential schools.

We learned more about the history and struggles of Canada's Aboriginal peoples in those few hours than in all our years of schooling.

After that incredible meeting, Atleo rolled up his sleeves and joined the construction team, as an honorary *fundi*, or carpenter, building the new school alongside the locals.

Helping us build a school was a fitting activity—we share with Atleo a passion for education. He notes that 200 First Nations communities in Canada still lack schools.

When we spoke with Atleo about who he is and what he does, one theme emerged again and again: raising consciousness. He is on a mission to increase awareness about the historic inequalities his people have faced—and the consequences that endure—because he believes that education spurs action. Atleo wants Aboriginal families to benefit equally from social programs that other Canadians enjoy, and communities to receive their fair share from the bountiful natural resources on Aboriginal lands. The more people are conscious of those challenges, the more they will want to join First Nations in working cooperatively to find solutions.

That is why Chief Atleo became a Patron of We Day, and a guiding force in Free The Children's We Stand Together campaign to bring together Aboriginal and non-Aboriginal people in a shared learning experience.

"In our language we have a phrase that says EVERYONE IS CONNECTED. All people are one and should be respected."

—SHAWN ATLEO

KENYAN BOYS CHOIR
THE CHORUS

The Kenyan Boys Choir started so students from underprivileged backgrounds could raise money to afford school fees. We met Davyd Chege when he was singing his way through interior design school and working as an intern in Free The Children's Nairobi office. When the group offered to perform for us, we'd never heard of the Kenyan Boys Choir, but soon the boys were serenading Free The Children's visiting volunteers around the campfire at Me to We's Bogani camp in Kenya.

Just months after their performance at Bogani, the choir was in Washington singing at US President Barack Obama's 2009 inauguration—not that we can take any credit for that.

Feeling pretty confident after their presidential performance, the Kenyan Boys Choir met The Tenors, a Canadian vocal group who'd come to Kenya to visit Free The Children's projects. With 25 choir members and the four tenors crammed into one living room for a vocal introduction, the Kenyans performed first, then looked to the Canadians, wondering what their four voices could do. The Tenors performed Leonard Cohen's "Hallelujah," leaving half of the choir in tears.

The choir has since teamed up with other artists, including UK singer Ellie Goulding and Nelly Furtado, at We Day or in Kenya. International musical collaboration is one of the unintended We Day perks. At We Day Toronto 2011, the choir joined Furtado onstage to sing her hit "Powerless," our favorite version of the song.

JAMES ORBINSKI
THE GOOD DOCTOR

Dr. James Orbinski is one of our greatest unsung heroes; the only Canadian since Prime Minister Lester B. Pearson in 1957 to hold the Nobel Peace Prize in his very capable, and lifesaving, hands.

In 1999, as Médecins Sans Frontières' international president, Orbinski accepted the award on behalf of MSF for its pioneering approach to medical humanitarianism, particularly for its act of witnessing, which refers to aid workers making the atrocities they observe known to the public.

Craig was a student at the University of Toronto when he came to know Orbinski, a Senior Fellow with the university's Massey College. They would sometimes sit in the garden outside the Munk School of Global Affairs and talk about international politics.

Orbinski helped build a celebrated global organization. Craig had a small organization with big dreams.

Craig hung on his every word, as Orbinski shared stories of his many missions for MSF. Among them, he was medical co-coordinator in Baidoa, Somalia, during the civil war and famine of 1992–1993. And he was MSF's Head of Mission in Kigali during the 1994 Rwandan genocide.

Orbinski told Craig of the feelings of futility that overwhelmed his work as a doctor in Rwanda, where he'd patch Tutsis up, only to watch them walk out the door to be slaughtered by waiting Hutus.

One day, a mother came in cradling a small child to her chest. She asked if Orbinski could "fix" the toddler. The mother held her child's severed head in her other hand.

It's difficult to imagine how he moved beyond the horror.

Orbinski is now a scholar, humanitarian, and global medicine specialist. When we had a chance to interview him, he spoke of the dedication and hard work needed to become skilled at something. But that is not all that is needed. "Discipline, focus, and push your own limits. And when you do, do it with a full heart."

Orbinski has graced the We Day stage several times. In September 2012, he introduced his hero, retired Lieutenant-General Romeo Dallaire. We Day is like that; it brings heroes together.

"Who is my hero? Anyone who has the courage to go through his or her fears and CREATE A BETTER WORLD."

—JAMES ORBINSKI

PINBALL CLEMONS
THE UNSTOPPABLE FORCE

The NFL's loss was our gain. After a stint with the Kansas City Chiefs, Michael Clemons—who would arguably become the Canadian Football League's most dynamic and popular player—stormed Toronto. With his relatively diminutive size and extraordinary balance, the 5-foot-6 running back and kick returner was nicknamed Pinball, perpetually bouncing off defenders.

Growing up watching him play, we marveled at his skill. He simply never gave up—and that resonated with us. Over the course of his 12-year playing career with the Toronto Argonauts, he won the Grey Cup, numerous MVP awards, and racked up amazing numbers. But you don't have to be a football fan to know Clemons brings real energy to everything he does.

The Florida native is now the Argos' vice-chair, and he is forever enriching his adopted home. A socially conscious entrepreneur, he started a reading program, launched his namesake foundation for disadvantaged youth, and leveraged his massive presence to become an incredible motivational speaker.

His involvement with Free The Children began when he and his wife, Diane, traveled with us to see our projects in Kenya.

"Children in third world countries drown from things other than the water being too deep," Clemons told a group of young volunteers on that trip. "Helping to build a school provides the structure for teaching and understanding. When you build a school, you are actually pulling kids out of the water."

After that trip, Clemons decided to reach into the water too—to help build schoolrooms where they were needed most. He vowed to build 31 schools, representing the number on his Argos jersey, plus 100 more. We were thrilled but somewhat skeptical, particularly when a five-year deadline was tabled.

But Clemons was determined. By hosting countless gala dinners, to creating specially-designed T-shirts, the proceeds of which went to school building, he surpassed expectations. In just three years, we built 152 schoolrooms together.

Clemons always has a goal line in sight: whether it's addressing gang violence, promoting scholarships for underprivileged students, or acting as a role model.

"Young people, if you were running the world, it would be a better place," he once told the We Day crowd. "The fact is, as people, we truly are better together."

There's nothing Clemons can't tackle.

"If young people ran the world, we'd have a kinder, more COMPASSIONATE world."

—PINBALL CLEMONS

SYDNEY BROUILLARD-COYLE
THE FUTURE PRIME MINISTER

W̶e hope to one day vote Sydney into office, but in the meantime, she's proving that children are not just the future—they are the present.

Like hundreds of thousands of students, the 12-year-old from Essex, Ontario, earned her way to We Day by committing to one local and one global service action. Her spark to act came when she was nine, after meeting a man named Richard at a local clothing cupboard. "His clothes were in tatters: a ripped T-shirt, shorts, and sandals," she recalled. It was October. Richard was so grateful for the clothing he received. She wondered why he had so little. "No human being should have to live this way."

She started growing fruits and vegetables for a local women's shelter. And she became more vocal about the issues that troubled her. When we heard she'd also written an inspiring speech, we invited her to deliver it at We Day events across the country.

WHEN I'M PRIME MINISTER

I have a dream that in 40 years I will be elected Prime Minister of Canada. Once I am Prime Minister, a few global issues will instantly be addressed. First of all, kids trying to make a difference will not be pushed aside, but rather encouraged to fulfill their calling. Because I know that children can make a difference.

We are born with a spark inside of us and it's our duty to light our sparks and turn them into a flame, and keep it going. That spark represents our passion, the issue that angers us the most. Once everyone's spark is turned to a flame, then together we can approach the local and global issues, and resolve them once and for all. Ignite your spark so that we can make a difference together.

Look around you! There are thousands of empowered youth right here, right now. The power in this room is simply incredible because everyone believes they can make a difference and it's true. But one thing that we have proved just by being here is that children are not just the future, they are the present too. The people here, this is just the beginning. You are not alone in this. We are in this together.

SYDNEY BROUILLARD-COYLE, WE DAY 2013

PHILIPPE COUSTEAU
THE DEEP DIVER

Philippe Cousteau refuses to watch environmental disasters from the shoreline. In 2010, he plunged into the Gulf of Mexico to investigate the impact of the Deepwater Horizon oil spill off the Louisiana coast. He strapped on his scuba gear to see the effects of the slick black water on the fragile ecosystem that lies deep below the surface.

The grandson of the legendary environmentalist and explorer Jacques Cousteau, it's not hard to see where Cousteau gets his passion for the natural world. At We Day he spoke of the environmental tragedies he's witnessed, but explained that these challenges are not insurmountable. He believes that education is the key to saving our planet. As a special correspondent for CNN International, Cousteau spreads the word about environmental protection. And, together with his sister Alexandra, he created EarthEcho International to empower youth to take action to conserve water and restore the planet.

Inspired by the young people at We Day, Cousteau reaffirms his belief that his grandfather's dream can become reality: that every child has the right to walk on green grass, drink from a babbling freshwater brook, and breathe clean air.

"*In the face of all the challenges and all the disasters and bad news there is tremendous* HOPE."

—PHILIPPE COUSTEAU

JENNIFER HUDSON
THE VOICE

Jennifer Hudson doesn't just perform; she holds court. In the closing moments of We Day Toronto 2012, Hudson sang her version of Leonard Cohen's "Hallelujah," building up from an intimate whisper to a final chorus that shook the 18,000-seat stadium, awash in twinkling blue as LED lights marked the beat.

Everyone was moved, and we know it had little to do with the lighting, the massive crowd, or the fact that it is Craig's favorite song of all time. Hudson is captivating, even at sound check without a proper audience.

We have just one rehearsal prior to each We Day event, making it a day fraught with chaos. Scripts are edited; prompters are moved, then moved again; mics are labeled; speeches are timed. Everyone is frantic with the thought of having to pull off a minor miracle the next day. But late in the afternoon on We Day Toronto's eve, Hudson took the stage, and manic motion ceased. She sang two songs to prep for her set, and then requested time for a third song that wasn't in the show. Hudson recorded Tina Turner's version of "Proud Mary" as a surprise present for her aunt's birthday, and brought a bit of Motown feeling back in a private concert for We Day staff.

Hudson is involved with organizations that work to stop violence against women, support cancer research, and protect the environment, among others. The Hudson-King Foundation for Families of Slain Victims was created in 2008 to honor Hudson's mother, brother, and nephew, killed that year in a tragic shooting. In every way, Hudson uses her voice to carry a positive message.

"To me this room is filled with ANGELS."

—JENNIFER HUDSON

"It can't be done: the four most DESTRUCTIVE words in the English language."

—LORNE SEGAL

LORNE SEGAL
THE BUSINESS OF COMMUNITY

Vancouver-based real-estate developer and philanthropist Lorne Segal is a hometown hero. As the long-time Chair of the Courage To Come Back Awards, an initiative in partnership with the Coast Mental Health Foundation in his home province of British Columbia, Segal supports local residents and raises awareness about mental health. The annual awards honor individuals living with mental illness and overcoming its many challenges, from addiction to underemployment—and thriving as outreach workers or documentary filmmakers, to cite a few examples. There's a special category for youth; past recipients have come back from poverty, abuse, or homelessness.

Segal has also inspired his children to take action—the family supports causes that bring them together. After a family trip to Kenya, the Segals saw that goats—by producing milk and offspring for sale—could provide alternative income and sustainability. So Segal organized a goat fundraiser in Vancouver, with help from wife Melita and their children, Matthew and Chanelle, then 15 and 17, who emceed the event. "Changing the World, One Goat at a Time" raised funds to provide 908 goats for families in developing communities around the world.

That passion for inspiring the next generation spurred Segal's interest in We Day. After the inaugural We Day event in Toronto in 2007, Segal told us about his experience. "There were thousands of kids screaming for social change. I had never seen anything like that before." Among them were Matthew and Chanelle. Segal—as event chair—and his family, helped bring We Day to Vancouver and continues to be our champion.

K'NAAN
THE TROUBADOUR

In the immediate aftermath of the 2010 earthquake in Haiti, we traveled to the Caribbean nation to help with relief efforts. Amid the devastation, we witnessed a group of determined Haitians climb to the summit of a rubble pile that was once the National Palace. At its summit they proudly hung the Haitian flag on a mangled fence. It was a gesture of defiance and human strength that reminded us of the spirit and optimism in our friend K'naan's song, "Wavin' Flag."

The song depicts his own deeply moving refugee story: his struggles with poverty and fear in war-torn Somalia, followed by feelings of displacement in a new country. But it also strikes a universal chord of redemption and hope.

Born in Mogadishu, K'naan Warsame grew up in a neighborhood known as the "River of Blood." He and his family miraculously escaped the 1991 civil war on the last commercial flight out of the country. They first landed in New York City before settling with relatives in Toronto, but wound up in one of its roughest neighborhoods. Life as a newcomer in Canada's largest city was not easy.

The young K'naan struggled for acceptance, often clashing with the police. Surrounded by violence and killing, he watched friends die needlessly or end up in jail. It would have been easy to give up hope and follow his friends down the same destructive path, but he held onto a dream. He told us that it was "a vision for a better idea of self, better idea of the world, better idea of the future," that kept him alive. As a means of salvation, K'naan turned to music and paved a different path for himself.

It has been amazing to watch his meteoric rise to international stardom. He first performed at We Day Vancouver 2009. A year later in Toronto, the entire crowd sang every word of "Wavin' Flag" along with K'naan in a performance that brought the house down.

Following the earthquake in Haiti, we proudly teamed up with K'naan and a group of recording artists, from Nelly Furtado and Drake to The Tenors and Justin Bieber, as they remixed "Wavin' Flag" for a charity single. The proceeds went to a collection of charitable organizations, including Free The Children, and raised more than a million dollars for Haiti relief.

"I always had some kind of a DREAMER quality. In my life, even under tough conditions and circumstances, I never really thought of the world as a hopeless place."

—K'NAAN

MICHAËLLE JEAN
HER HEART AND SOUL

Born in the Haitian capital of Port-au-Prince, Michaëlle Jean immigrated to Canada as a child, fleeing Haiti's oppressive government with her family. Throughout her life, she maintained a special bond with the people and cultures of both her native land and her adopted home. In Canada, she worked with battered women and helped establish emergency shelters across the country. She became a respected journalist on CBC Television, then served as Canada's Governor General from 2005 to 2010. Afterward, she established the Michaëlle Jean Foundation to support arts programming for underserved youth. The compassion and grace she brings to each effort seems to unite an otherwise diverse set of passions.

When the devastating earthquake struck Haiti on January 12, 2010, leveling most of Port-au-Prince, Jean delivered a heartfelt and tearful speech that moved many Canadians to support relief efforts. She was subsequently appointed UNESCO's Special Envoy for Haiti to spearhead an initiative to restore the country's education system and protect its culture and heritage. With her warmth and empathy, Jean captured the hearts of people in Canada, in Haiti, and around the world—including ours.

"*Not only do young people CARE, but young people want to make a difference here and now, for more vibrant, healthy, viable communities at home and abroad.*"

—MICHAËLLE JEAN

PAUL MARTIN
THE PUBLIC SERVANT

Most people know Paul Martin as the 21st Prime Minister of Canada, but we've come to know him as an advocate for the rights of Aboriginal peoples. After his retirement from politics he could have taken pause or pursued any number of passions, but seeking equal opportunities for First Nations, Métis, and Inuit has always been close to his heart.

As Prime Minister, Martin recognized the inadequacy of federal funding for Aboriginal education and was frustrated by the general lack of understanding of Aboriginal issues among politicians. In response, he endorsed the Kelowna Accord in 2005, which would have invested $5 billion over ten years in education and social welfare programs for Aboriginal Canadians. But before it could be officially adopted, Martin's government lost power and the bill died. Discouraged but not defeated, Martin continues to fight for what he believes is just.

In 2008, he created the Martin Aboriginal Education Initiative to improve the quality of education for Aboriginal Canadians through a variety of projects and initiatives. One of those initiatives, We Stand Together, is a program designed in partnership with Free The Children to start the public conversation about Aboriginal culture, traditions, and history, and to address the unique challenges faced by Aboriginal peoples.

Talking with Martin, we quickly discovered our common belief that education must be at the root of change and that there are desperate shortcomings in Aboriginal education. "What we're trying to do is fill those gaps in terms of literacy, in terms of numeracy," Martin explained to us. "We're trying to provide them with as close as we can possibly get to the same education that most Canadians have and to which they are entitled."

Martin reminds us that we don't have to look to distant continents to find injustice and inequality.

"We cannot speak about our VALUES unless we're prepared to put those values to work."

—PAUL MARTIN

SHAQUILLE O'NEAL
THE BIG HEART

Growing up in New Jersey, Shaquille O'Neal towered over his classmates. "I was always ashamed of being bigger," he told us. But he adapted. "I was a big kid, but I created a style—to get people to recognize me for who I am."

Quite the style. He became one of the greatest basketball players to ever grace the court.

This 15-time NBA All-Star and four-time NBA champion attributes his determination to the lessons his father taught him. O'Neal was never allowed to rest on his laurels. His father pushed him to set goals, achieve them, and then set new challenges. In this way O'Neal developed self-confidence and learned to defy his critics. To this day, he gives his father his trophies—even his four NBA Championship rings.

After retiring in 2011, he channeled his willpower into humanitarian work and educational pursuits. He teamed up with the Boys and Girls Club of America, the gay-rights watchdog GLAAD, and has worked with us at We Day and on our We are Silent campaign. In 2012, O'Neal earned a doctorate degree in Leadership and Education from Barry University in Miami, Florida—proving wrong those pundits who thought althetes were all brawn and no brains.

"You can't play basketball forever," he told us. "But you can always educate yourself. You can always better yourself. You can always better someone else's life." This belief was behind his message to the crowd at We Day when he urged them:"Be leaders, not followers!"

"Young people need to realize that the world is theirs. They have visions that they can actually walk up to and touch if they BELIEVE, if they stay leaders not followers, if they stay out of trouble. My mother and father preached that to me my whole life. You can do whatever you want to do."

—SHAQUILLE O'NEAL

141

SARAH MCLACHLAN
THE POWER OF SONG

Few artists have been as successful and giving as singer-songwriter Sarah McLachlan. She topped the charts with platinum records and collected multiple Grammy and Juno awards, then used her famous voice to call out to those in need. Rather than shoot a conventional music video for "World on Fire," McLachlan donated all but $15 of the $150,000 budget to various charities and then used the video to explain how the money would instead benefit communities around the world. She leant her hit song "Angel" to help raise $30 million for the American Society for the Prevention of Cruelty to Animals. We were thrilled to have her perform both songs at We Day.

McLachlan is a bona fide music industry pioneer. In the 1990s, she shattered gender stereotypes with the massively successful all-female music festival Lilith Fair. Today, she uses the power of song and sound to make a difference in the lives of underserved and at-risk young people, offering free music education through the Sarah McLachlan School of Music in East Vancouver. We are fans of McLachlan's big talent and even bigger heart.

"The energy out there was incredible. Thousands of passionate kids just having an amazing time. The SPIRIT was wonderful."

—SARAH MCLACHLAN

AL GORE
THE ECO WARRIOR

When we arrived at the official residence of the Vice President of the United States, metal barricades disappeared into the ground to allow our car to pass, and then we were given a pat down by the Secret Service. It's not an exaggeration to say we were a bit scared to meet Albert Gore Jr.—second-in-command of the most powerful nation on Earth. Then the door to his home swung open…and we were ushered in by the smell of homemade oatmeal raisin cookies.

His wife, Tipper, served them to us on a fancy tray—with milk. We were too nervous to eat. Almost. They were delicious. Then we sat with Gore, his wife and three of their four children, who matched us in age. We finally understood what this "top level" visit in 1996 was all about. Gore asked us for milk and cookies because he wanted to hear about Craig's fact-finding mission to meet child laborers in South Asia, and about Marc's early actions to protect the environment with home-brewed cleaners. But mostly, he wanted us to speak to his children about our efforts to raise awareness for child rights and preserve the environment, and to talk with them about their own budding passions.

This was early days, before Gore won acclaim for *An Inconvenient Truth*, and a Nobel Peace Prize jointly awarded in 2007 to the Intergovernmental Panel on Climate Change. We chatted for two hours; he told us his drive to serve others came from his parents, "who are heroes to me." He clearly had the same impact on his kids. That day, he became much more to us

than the Vice President of the United States; he became a dad. It was one of life's surreal experiences, especially when Tipper banged out a rhythm on her drum kit.

This meeting led to a long-term friendship with Gore, a committed environmentalist, and one of the most sought-after speakers at We Day. He has been involved with environmental issues since 1976, when the then-28-year-old rookie congressman held the first congressional hearings on climate change, and co-sponsored hearings on toxic waste and global warming.

He told us that making change is not simple, the path rarely clear. "We face the same choices over and over again, between the hard right and the easy wrong."

From the We Day stage, he delivers a message to the next generation: protect the planet before the ice caps melt, the ocean levels rise, and water and food shortages imperil our population. "The will to act is a renewable resource. It lives in your heart: wake it up, wake it up in yourselves. Rise up to make this world what it should be."

This is a man, and a father, who has not retired quietly from public life, but continues to encourage young people to help build the world they will inherit.

ON OUR MISSION

When I was 12 or 13 years old, I was inspired by a former president of my country, John F. Kennedy. He issued a challenge to put a person on the moon and bring him back safely within ten years. I thought that was so cool. And yet I heard many older people say that it was a mistake for him to make that commitment. It will cost so much money. And it's so hard. It's never been done before. We shouldn't even try something like that.

Eight years and two months later Neil Armstrong and Buzz Aldrin set foot on the surface of the moon. And the moment they did so, in NASA's mission control, a great cheer went up. And you know, the average age of the systems engineers in mission control that day was 26 years old. Think about that. It means that when they heard that challenge their average age was 18 years old. And they decided to commit themselves to be a part of that great journey; to be a part of succeeding in that unbelievable mission.

We have a mission now! Together we can save the future, free the children, make this world a better place! In the future, if they look around and see solar energy, wind energy, more efficient technologies, new designs for buildings and cities, and millions of new jobs, they will have hope in their hearts that the world is getting to be a better place. I want them to look back and ask the question: "How did they rise up to make the world a better place? How did they find the commitment in their hearts to do what was necessary to save the future?"

AL GORE, WE DAY 2012

"*NATURE* doesn't do bailouts. You can't repeal the laws of physics."

—AL GORE

"I look up to, respect, admire, and am inspired by all of the COMMITMENT to service work right here in this room."

—MACKLEMORE

MACKLEMORE
THE TRENDSETTER

Ben Haggerty, more famously known as Macklemore, made it big paying homage to reasonably priced clothing. His "Thrift Shop" music video, a collaboration with Ryan Lewis, debuted on YouTube in 2012 and racked up over two hundred million views in just a few months. Macklemore's rotating video wardrobe includes Batman footie pajamas, an ugly Hawaiian shirt, sweaters last seen on TV dads in the 80s, and a vintage leopard mink—in the song, he claims it was 99 cents. He's credited with launching a mini cultural revolution, and not just because your grandpa's cardigans now have street cred. His song "Same Love" challenges homophobia in hip-hop culture, and has been called an anthem for tackling one of the foremost issues of equality in our time.

In "Thrift Shop," Seattle's own Macklemore sports a Seahawks T-shirt under a bleach-dyed denim vest. So it's fitting that Seahawks Head Coach Pete Carroll introduced Macklemore and Lewis as surprise guests at We Day Seattle.

Macklemore is somehow completely ridiculous and impossibly suave. But he told the We Day crowd not to focus on image: "It's so easy to get caught up in yourself and in your world, in what you're wearing. Get out of it and give back to others." Maybe his thrift shop rap is just a ruse to promote socially conscious habits.

LIZ MURRAY
THE STUDENT OF LIFE

Liz Murray overcame tremendous odds to go from "homeless to Harvard"—showing the limitless potential of the human spirit and serving as a remarkable example of what happens when you dream big.

Murray's childhood was bleak. The daughter of cocaine-addicted parents in the Bronx, there were drugs everywhere in her childhood home, but no food. At 15, Murray's HIV-positive mom died and her terminally ill father moved to a shelter, leaving her homeless. She rode the subways at night and ate from dumpsters. Murray imagined a better life.

"Growing up I was tough on myself," Murray told us after one of her many inspirational appearances at We Day. "I remember picturing that I was going to become this optimal person. I could even picture a pyramid, like I was rising up."

Murray saw education as the key to start climbing, finishing high school in just two years—while camping out in New York City parks. She went on to earn a scholarship from the *New York Times* and entered Harvard in 2000.

It was at Harvard that Marc, as an undergrad, first knew Murray. In fact everyone had heard of her: she had gained widespread respect and acceptance among her peers. Murray embraced the Harvard experience, and excelled. And she did so without a parent. Marc remembers the intense demands that were made more manageable by the support he received from home. Murray graduated with a BS in Psychology from Harvard University in June 2009.

Today as an inspirational speaker, and more importantly, as a mom, selflessness and hope are at the core of her message for young people—whether they are facing their own obstacles or seeking their role in changing the world.

"When you think of what you really want to create in this world, don't only think of yourself," Murray told us. "Think of your community, think of your world. If everyone has that mentality we can cultivate a culture of kindness and giving."

"It's better to LIGHT a candle than to curse the darkness."

—LIZ MURRAY

WANEEK HORN-MILLER
THE BRIDGE BUILDER

We were still quite young when conflict erupted in 1990 between Mohawks and the town of Oka, Quebec, over plans to build a golf course on top of sacred traditional burial grounds. As the situation escalated and the army was called in, we listened to our parents and teachers discuss and debate the crisis that became the focus of the nation. Like many, the iconic image of a masked Mohawk nose-to-nose with a Canadian soldier remains etched in our memory.

We remember, too, our shock upon hearing that a young Aboriginal girl, not much older than us, had been stabbed and nearly killed by a soldier during the crisis.

Fast forward 21 years to 2011, when we invited an inspiring Olympian and Aboriginal activist by the name of Waneek Horn-Miller to speak at We Day. We listened in awe as she shared her incredible story, and our jaws dropped as we made the connection—this was her! She was that girl we had heard about all those years before.

Horn-Miller and her three sisters were raised in the Mohawk community of Kahnawake by their mother, an Aboriginal rights activist, who taught them about perseverance, courage of conviction, and the importance of giving back.

After she was nearly killed during the historic events at Oka, Horn-Miller grappled with the anger and disillusionment she felt toward Canada and its treatment of Aboriginal peoples. With the help of sports—first competitive swimming, then water polo—she undertook a personal journey of forgiveness and reconciliation.

In 1999, she bore Canada's flag at the opening of the Pan Am Games in Winnipeg, and one year later she represented our country, co-captaining the women's water polo team at the Sydney Summer Olympics.

Horn-Miller agreed to go on a speaking tour with us to help non-Aboriginal youth gain a better understanding of both the past and present for Aboriginal peoples in Canada. Her words build bridges of understanding between cultures. "I need to get more people feeling the passion I do about my own people," she told us.

It is Aboriginal leaders like Waneek Horn-Miller who can show us the path on our collective journey to forgiveness, reconciliation, and cooperation between Aboriginal and non-Aboriginal people.

"The biggest part of being in a COMMUNITY is contribution."

—WANEEK HORN-MILLER

ROMÉO DALLAIRE
THE GENERAL

Roméo Dallaire was a career soldier, born of a military family. His skill, dedication, and leadership earned him the rank of Lieutenant-General in the Canadian Forces and command of such units as the First Canadian Division. In 1993 he received a commission that would change his life—Force Commander of the United Nations Assistance Mission in Rwanda. He was tasked with keeping the peace between Rwanda's two major ethnic groups, the Hutus and Tutsis.

Dallaire did his best to prevent the bloodshed that followed, and although his actions are credited with saving more than 32,000 lives, in the end he could not stop the systematic wholesale slaughter of an estimated 800,000 innocents.

We once visited a memorial for the victims of the Rwanda genocide outside Kigali. There were no professionally-produced displays and no documentary film projections. It was just a church—the site of a massacre that had been left exactly as it was. Blood still stained the walls and human remains littered the floor. A crushed skull lay near the altar. In a large shed nearby, piles of bones, sorted by type, made small mountains on tarps laid out on the floor.

The memory of that place, that visceral experience, still haunts us, and yet we realize we cannot comprehend the smallest fraction of the horror that Dallaire witnessed. Our hearts lurched as we listened to him recount his story at We Day.

Rwanda left Dallaire deeply scarred. He retired from the military with post-traumatic stress disorder, and nearly took his own life. Speaking with Dallaire since then, we have felt his sincere caring for everyone around him. But also, the bubbling anger that lies beneath—a fury at the world's inaction.

With heroic courage Dallaire has battled back from depression and now fights a new war—against the use of child soldiers. We understand the need. We've sat with child soldiers as they've spoken about their horrific lives, from the initiation rituals that pit them against other children, to the girls forced into sexual slavery. Dallaire's Child Soldiers Initiative raises global awareness about children caught up in conflict, and creates resources to help police and military peacekeepers protect their rights.

Every time Dallaire takes the We Day stage, he shocks and inspires young people to raise their voices. In his own words, he says he hopes to "instill in them the willingness to fight for human rights."

"*I hope that one day we will resolve the frictions of our differences without having to kill and having to destroy through* CONFLICT."

—ROMÉO DALLAIRE

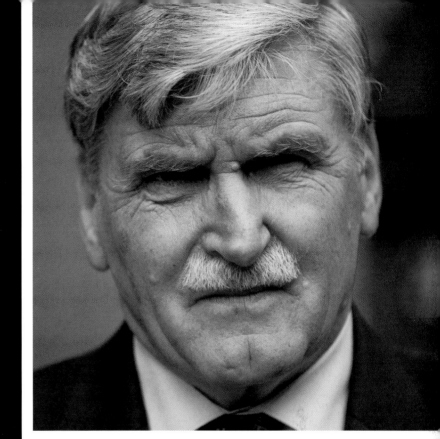

NINA DOBREV
SHE SCARES HUNGER

Actor Nina Dobrev saw poverty for the first time on a Me to We Trip to Kenya; when she was 17, she helped build a school in the rural Maasai Mara. But that was just the beginning of her journey with Free The Children.

Dobrev has been a supporter of We Day since its humble origins in 2007—our small staff had serious ambition, a semblance of a plan, and an adrenaline overload that only unabashed optimists can generate. Despite our opening jitters, she roused 7,500 youth at the inaugural We Day Toronto as an official Ambassador for Free The Children. She has since been back as co-host, and remains our spokesperson for the We Scare Hunger campaign, a food drive that has kids trick-or-treating for canned goods instead of candy on Halloween. It's part of her passion to end hunger in North America and around the world. Her "Hunger Bites" tee, designed with Me to We Style, supports programs that fight drought in East Africa. The tee is also a cheeky nod to her starring role in the hit series *The Vampire Diaries*.

"HUNGER BITES. And not just because I'm on a vampire show."

—NINA DOBREV

"*LOVE without action is meaningless. And action without love is irrelevant.*"

—DEEPAK CHOPRA

DEEPAK CHOPRA
THE GURU

Life raises some big questions. And when Deepak Chopra spoke to our young volunteers, he urged them to ask: Why am I here? What kind of world do I want to inherit? How will I help create that world? What is the meaning and purpose of my life? Who are my heroes and heroines in history, in mythology, in religion? He said we must live the answers.

The Indian-born American physician is a world-renowned pioneer in mind-body healing and perhaps the most famous practitioner of alternative medicine. He started his career on a conventional path, rising to become Chief of Staff at a Boston hospital. But after studying the traditional healing practices of Ayurveda with the Maharishi Mahesh Yogi, he took a road less traveled, at least in the West—devoting his life to Ayurveda and the connections between mind and body. He has written more than 64 books, including numerous *New York Times* bestsellers, with the hope of bringing his ideas into the mainstream. He is the go-to guru and spiritual advisor for many celebrities and world leaders.

At We Day he counseled self-exploration through service. He said "action without love is irrelevant." What we give to the world is who we become.

MARTIN SHEEN
A REBEL WITH A CAUSE

We once asked activist and acclaimed actor Martin Sheen how he felt before facing the We Day crowd, and his response surprised us. Public speaking is his mountain to climb.

"It is my Mount Kilimanjaro," he told us backstage at We Day. "As I stand there, my heart is pounding, my knees are shaking—all of my insecurities are boiling over the top looking for any excuse to have this cup pass from me."

One of Hollywood's most respected performers, with more than 100 films to his credit, is like so many others in North America: he fears public speaking. But he seizes the challenge.

"If I don't come here and I don't speak, I have stunted my growth. It is the only way I can come to know myself."

And when he's conquered his fear and walked off the stage: "It's a real joy."

No one could imagine that Sheen was wracked by self-doubt when he powerfully proclaimed to 18,000 young people: "One heart with courage—is a majority!" Or when he encouraged the audience to take on the responsibility of caring for each other and the world—something he has been personally committed to since he was a teenager, like many in the crowd.

Sheen's path to acting and activism is unique.

Born in Dayton, Ohio, to immigrant parents struggling to make a go of it in America, Sheen learned early about the painful inequalities between the privileged and the less fortunate. At 14, he organized a strike of the caddies at the local country club where he worked.

From there, his values evolved during the turbulent 1960s, when young people protested war abroad and racial and gender discrimination at home. In particular, Sheen found inspiration in the lives of Bobby Kennedy, Mahatma Gandhi, and the great civil rights crusader Martin Luther King Jr. It was in these formative years that Sheen first developed the inkling for social justice issues and non-violent activism that would become a life-long passion.

Sheen has dedicated his energy to fighting for human rights, nuclear disarmament, environmental protection, and has campaigned tirelessly to eradicate poverty in the developing world. His fearless commitment to these causes knows no bounds; he has been arrested more than 60 times for his participation in public protests.

As an actor, he burst onto the scene in the 1970s with critically acclaimed performances in *Badlands* and *Apocalypse Now*. But he didn't stop there. Spanning six decades—and showing no signs of slowing down—his career highlights include *Wall Street* (co-starring his son Charlie) and *The Departed*.

metro

Martin Sheen
at We Day!

His stint as the judgemental father on the hit comedy *Anger Management* began in 2012. Before that, he was America's favorite president—and ours—on television, anyway. His role as fictional Commander in Chief Josiah Bartlet on *The West Wing* introduced Sheen to a new generation of TV viewers and garnered him six Emmy Award nominations and a Golden Globe.

Sheen is a regular in the We Day line-up—delivering, with equal parts charm and passion, some of the most captivating and moving speeches heard on our stage.

We love Sheen's wonderful sense of humor and his humility. We once asked him what he'd like his legacy to be, and he quipped: "Absolutely none. The sooner I'm forgotten, the better."

His extraordinary body of work, both on and off the screen, is inspirational—reminding us that idealism is ageless. He will not be forgotten.

"*Acting is what I do for a living, but ACTIVISM is what I do to stay alive.*"

—MARTIN SHEEN

BETTY WILLIAMS
"AN ORDINARY HOUSEWIFE"

When Betty Williams garnered her first headlines, the press described her as a mere mother—an ordinary housewife. It was meant to be pejorative, but she embraced and redefined those labels. She became peacekeeper, protestor, and role model. After all, don't all mothers take up these tasks? Williams just did it on the world stage.

She became the most famous "housewife" in the world in 1977 when she was named a co-recipient, with Mairead Corrigan, of the Nobel Peace Prize for their work to end the "Troubles" in Northern Ireland. Williams also became a beacon of hope for anyone who wants to change the world but isn't a politician or statesman.

Williams stepped forward after witnessing the death of three children on August 10, 1976, when they were hit by a car whose driver, an Irish Republican Army fugitive, was fatally shot by British authorities. Within two days of the tragic event, Williams had gathered 6,000 signatures on a petition for peace. Together with Corrigan, she organized a peace march to the graves of the children, which was attended by 10,000 Protestant and Catholic women. The peaceful march was disrupted by members of the IRA, who accused them of being dupes of the British. The following week, Williams and Corrigan again led a march—this time with 35,000 strong. As momentum continued to build, Williams proved the persuasive power of an ordinary citizen.

She became a We Day favorite when she asked 18,000 people to stand and give their neighbor a hug. When we interviewed her later, she declared: "I have never met an ordinary housewife. Have you?"

She proposed that the biggest killer in our world is apathy—the bystanders who won't intervene because it's "none of my business." We should make the world's many challenges our business, she said. And through her example, she shows that one person can make a huge difference. She advised us, memorably, "Be an absolute idealist. And when somebody tells you you're wrong…If you can non-violently spit in their eye—do it!"

"Fear is contagious, but so is COURAGE."

—BETTY WILLIAMS

ELLEN JOHNSON SIRLEAF
THE IRON LADY OF LIBERIA

In 2010, Liberian president Ellen Johnson Sirleaf generously welcomed us into her home for a meeting over breakfast. As she gave us a quick tour, she pointed out several simple, framed puzzles that decorate her walls. She assembled these puzzles over the many years she spent in forced exile for defying Liberia's military dictatorships in the name of justice and democracy. Completing the puzzles taught her patience—a lesson she practices as she works to rebuild her fractured nation.

Born in the Liberian capital of Monrovia, she was married at 17 and four years later, in 1961, traveled to the US with her husband. The marriage didn't last, but she took advantage of the educational opportunities available. Armed with a Master of Public Administration from Harvard University, she returned to Liberia to enter government service. After a military coup in 1980, Johnson Sirleaf's open criticism of the new government's policies landed her in prison twice, before she fled the country—narrowly escaping execution.

The next 20 years would be defined by attempted returns to Liberia to work for her people, while she established an international reputation in exile as an economist. In 1997, she returned and ran for president against the infamous dictator Charles Taylor, who charged her with treason, forcing her into exile once more. In 2003, Taylor stepped down after losing a violent and bloody civil war, and Johnson Sirleaf returned for good, eventually becoming the first woman elected head of state in Africa.

She inherited a nation on the verge of economic collapse, plagued by vicious internal divisions. Determined to make democracy work, she feels Liberia is on the path to recovery. "I'd say what we've accomplished is the restoration of hope," she explained to us. "Hope in people who now see that they have a life, that they can be whatever they want to be in an environment that will give them the opportunity to do so."

When our breakfast with President Johnson Sirleaf came to an end, she returned to the puzzle metaphor when reflecting on her life's work: "I will not finish it," she explained, "but I will have put all the essential pieces in place so that whoever follows me will be able then to bring it all together into one great mosaic."

One of the essential pieces is her unwavering commitment to improving the lives of women, for which she was jointly awarded the 2011 Nobel Peace Prize.

"Every time you leap over a barrier, every time you OVERCOME an obstacle, it re-energizes you and you set the goal a bit higher."

—ELLEN JOHNSON SIRLEAF

THE TENORS
VIRTUOSOS

When our good friend and music management mogul Jeffrey Latimer signed on to co-chair We Day Toronto, we crossed our fingers that he would deliver outstanding musical acts. Our superstition paid off.

He introduced us to The Tenors—a vocal quartet breaking new ground with a mixture of opera and pop. Formerly known as The Canadian Tenors, Fraser Walters, Clifton Murray, Victor Micallef, and Remigio Pereira reinvented the classical tenor genre, establishing the group as a national treasure with global credentials.

Since first appearing at We Day in 2008, they have recorded three platinum-selling records, performed at the opening ceremonies for the 2010 Winter Olympics in Vancouver, graced the stage at Carnegie Hall, and sat down for tea with the Queen of England after performing at her Diamond Jubilee at Windsor Castle in London. They have earned the right to pick and choose their performance venues, and we are honored that they continue to make We Day a highlight of their tour schedule.

They first sang at We Day to inspire young people, but soon discovered the energy and passion of the young people inspired them as well. Deeply moved by the experience, they penned "Free The Children"—a We Day anthem of hope and promise. For sharing their virtuoso talent with us and always answering our call, we sing the praises of the incomparable Tenors.

FREE THE CHILDREN

Freedom
Lead them to freedom

We are young and we are free
We are here 'cause we believe
In our hearts we hold the key
To change the world from Me to We

Freedom
Let us free the children
And lead them to freedom

Freedom
Lead them to freedom

What we do and what we say
Can heal the wounds of yesterday
We make a promise and we pray
It's up to us to be the change

THE TENORS

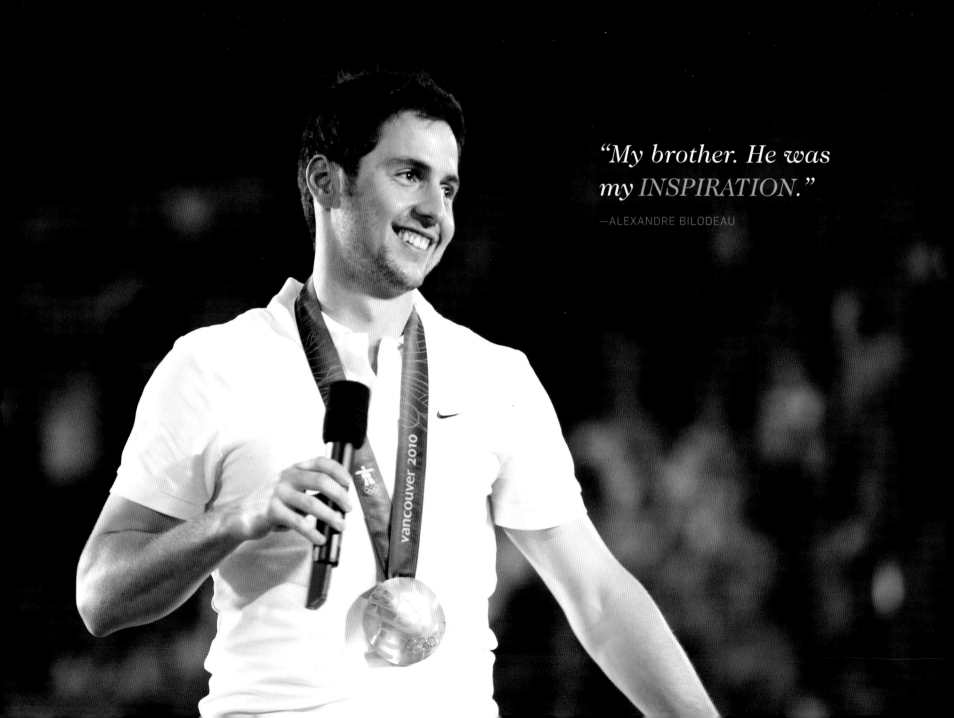

"My brother. He was my INSPIRATION."

—ALEXANDRE BILODEAU

ALEXANDRE BILODEAU
THE MOGUL

On a clear, crisp winter night in 2010, Montreal's Alexandre Bilodeau skied the race of his life, and made Olympic history. Sticking a flawless back double full jump followed by an equally perfect back iron cross, Bilodeau flew down the Cypress Mountain mogul course to become the first Canadian to win Olympic gold on home soil. Bilodeau set the pace for Canadian athletes as they marched on to collect the most gold medals of any country at the 2010 Winter Games in Vancouver.

Cheering him on was Bilodeau's older brother, Frédéric: his biggest fan and main source of inspiration. Frédéric was born with cerebral palsy, and doctors predicted he wouldn't walk beyond age ten. Yet, there he was at 28, at the base of the hill—still on his feet. Moved by his brother's determination to beat the odds, Bilodeau pushed himself to the limit during grueling training sessions. And boy did it pay off.

Bilodeau has used his Olympic fame to help others like Frédéric by supporting the Canadian Association of Paediatric Health Centres' research into cerebral palsy, and donating his gold medal-winning skis to raise money for Three To Be, a charity dedicated to assisting children with neurological disorders. We were immensely proud to have Bilodeau speak at We Day, with Olympic gold around his neck.

JONAS BROTHERS
SIBLING PHILANTHROPY

The Jonas Brothers made their first We Day appearance in a video message in Toronto in 2009. We thought it was loud when they appeared on screen. But when Joe, Nick, and Kevin burst from backstage—the video was a ruse—to surprise the audience with a live performance, they took the stage to deafening screams. You could barely hear the brothers above the thousands of voices singing along.

These brothers have earned the fanfare. Nick began performing on Broadway at the ripe old age of seven. As a group, they've starred in Disney movies, made multiple albums with record-breaking sales, performed at the White House, and toured the world.

Not bad for three kids from the Jersey Shore.

While New Jersey's pier was made famous by the debauchery of reality television, the Jonas family couldn't be further from the binge-drinking, bar-fighting stereotype. Sons of a former pastor, the brothers are strong Evangelical Christians, homeschooled by their mother. They were raised to care deeply about making the world a better place. As such, they've rocked out at charity galas, attended foundation dinners, and raised funds for more than two dozen charities—for causes ranging from mosquito nets to prevent malaria, to Alzheimer's research, and music education. Not to mention their work with us.

Middle brother, Joe, designed the eco-friendly, sweatshop-free "Mantra Tee" for Me to We Style, with proceeds supporting Free The Children. He rocked the shirt to co-host and perform at We Day Toronto 2011. The band was also inspired to start their own foundation, Change for the Children, an umbrella charity that supports the American Diabetes Association and the Make-a-Wish Foundation, among other causes. That's an impressive gene pool.

"I've always felt a responsibility to give back. I've traveled to amazing places and met incredible people, all because I've gotten INVOLVED."

—JOE JONAS

MARTIN LUTHER KING III
THE LEGACY

Martin Luther King III, eldest son of civil rights leader Martin Luther King Jr., embraces the legacy of his family name. He told us, "If I can use my name, my influence, to create what my father would have called, 'the beloved community,' then I've done something good."

But first he had to learn to forgive. "I lost my father at ten, my uncle at eleven. My grandmother was gunned down in the church when I was sixteen. So I had a lot of trauma in my life," he told us. "But what I came to—and I had to learn how to forgive—was to love myself. You really can't love other selves if you don't first love you."

His love extends beyond himself and his family, to his community and the greater world. He expresses this love through service. Following in his father's footsteps, he took up the struggle for racial equality in America—in 1997, with the Southern Christian Leadership Conference, the civil rights organization founded by his father four decades earlier. He now heads The King Center in Atlanta, dedicated to advancing his father's mission.

King has also done an enormous amount of good as an elected official, civil rights advocate, and community activist. To promote goodness, he believes we have to nurture empathy in others.

"People don't want sympathy, they want empathy. They want you to feel with them, to be engaged," he told us. "They also want to do something positive. It doesn't matter what it is, it can be something very small or it can be something that becomes huge."

King keeps faith in his father's dream for a more equal and compassionate world. To mark the 50th anniversary of the March on Washington—the day in 1963 that "I have a dream" echoed around the world—King joined the We Day tour and spoke to more than one hundred thousand young people at events across North America about equality and compassion.

"The dream remains unfulfilled, but it is still very much alive."

"When you love your COMMUNITY, you don't accept poverty, you don't accept hunger, you don't accept bullying."

—MARTIN LUTHER KING III

ROBIN WISZOWATY
THE TRAVELER

Robin Wiszowaty stood on the water's edge in the small Ghanaian village of Asemkow, watching fishermen play tug of war with the ocean, hauling in their nets and turning over their boats to serve as benches for a community meeting on the shore. The women sat in the shade of a nearby tree, children on laps or at their feet.

In that meeting, and the many that would come later, Wiszowaty and her team carefully cultivated relationships with elders, government officials, and the Chief. Together, they determined where the community's first Free The Children school would be built. Children marked the outline of the future classroom with stones, imagining the students who'd rush through it.

Growing these fledgling, precious relationships takes diplomacy and patience. Wiszowaty is a facilitator, mediator, and messenger for Free The Children. She's a cultural bridge between our partner communities in Africa and our volunteers in the West.

There's a proverb from the Central Highlands region of Kenya, *Kumagara ni Kuhinga*, which means "traveling is learning." It makes us think of Wiszowaty.

In 2002, at age 21, Wiszowaty left the gleaming strip malls, street grids, and suburban backyards of her hometown in Schaumburg, Illinois, for the wilds of rural Kenya. Looking back, she told us what led her there. Her idle teenage rebellion was more than angst; it was a vague restlessness, an unshakable feeling that she was missing something. She loved her family, had close friends, swam competitively, and joined her high school's student council. She didn't feel she belonged. "I was looking for something I couldn't articulate," she said. "I wanted to learn things I didn't know I needed to learn." Nothing kept her tethered to her life in Middle America.

Arriving in Kenya's Maasai Mara, Wiszowaty threw herself forcefully into culture shock through her university's exchange program and moved into a traditional *boma*, a mud hut of cow dung and straw. She took one look at the humble dwelling, the cowhide she'd sleep on with her adoptive siblings, the bucket she'd bathe with, and fell in love, finding her home with her Maasai family. She immersed herself in the culture and learned the language over the course of a year.

Returning to Illinois was not so easy. The reverse culture shock was "intense and terrible," leaving her "holed up" in her room for days. When she did go out, she'd walk barefoot, carrying her shoes. She was overcome by the consumer values, frustrated at the wasteful habits and "naïve ignorance" of those around her.

Wiszowaty shared with us an important moment of clarity: "I realized it's not fair to judge others because they haven't had my experience. I need to share stories of hope and potential." She saw her travels as a privilege that comes with great responsibility. Her story longed to be told. Since then, as a Me to We speaker and author, her story has touched millions.

Today, we can't imagine that Wiszowaty would feel out of place anywhere. We know her by her gum boots, ankle-deep in mud from Kenya's long rains, balancing a jerry can of Mara River water on her back, walking alongside the Maasai mamas. We know her by her hushed conversations with village elders. We see school children run to her for an embrace or sit at her feet as she conspires with them in flawless Swahili. We see Wiszowaty at home in Africa. Then we watch her fly thousands of miles to captivate audiences in every We Day city across North America and the UK with the story of her incredible journey.

Wiszowaty has taught thousands of people, including us, about travel and adventure, about community and family, about learning and acceptance. This is how we know Wiszowaty. As someone who belongs, wherever she travels.

"With your help we can continue to break the cycle of POVERTY around the world."

—ROBIN WISZOWATY

IZZELDIN ABUELAISH
THE GAZA DOCTOR

The unthinkable private grief of Dr. Izzeldin Abuelaish unraveled very publicly on live television. He'd hoped to be witness to war in order to expose its senselessness—but not in this way.

The doctor had been acting as an informal Palestinian correspondent living in the Gaza Strip after most journalists had fled the war in late 2008 and 2009. He was sending updates via phone calls to his friend, Shlomi Eldar, a reporter for Israel's Channel. Then, a ground invasion turned Abuelaish's backyard into a war zone.

By the time the tanks reached his front door, Abuelaish and his family were holed up with no escape. Israeli shells bombarded his home, where his daughters: Aya, 14, Mayar, 15, and Bessan, 20, along with his niece, Noor, were hiding. The family was unreachable by ambulance, their home a mess of debris. Soldiers and potholes blocked the streets. Abuelaish called the only contact he could think of.

Eldar was taping a broadcast news segment in Tel Aviv when he took his friend's frantic call. Live on Israel's Channel 10, Abuelaish cried out in shock for his little girls, whose blows to the head were fatal. "My daughters, oh God, oh Allah, my daughters!" he cried. "I want to save them, to save them! But they are dead! What have we done?!" His hysterical screams are captured forever in video footage.

In the aftermath, Abuelaish refuses to be angry. As a doctor, a teacher, a speaker, and the founder of Daughters for Life, he shares his tragedy as a catalyst to promote peace and reconciliation. His foundation provides leadership development opportunities and access to education for girls throughout the Middle East—and it honors the memory of his daughters. Abuelaish spoke on a Peace Panel at We Day, alongside former child soldier Michel Chikwanine and Nobel Peace Prize Laureate Betty Williams. He pointedly addressed the crowd of young people, many the same ages as his daughters when they were killed. "Girls are our potential," he said. "They are our future."

He called on the girls in the crowd to be leaders and allow others to follow. He told them never to underestimate themselves and never to give up. "Nothing is impossible. The only impossible thing, I've learned, is to return my daughters back. Anything else in life you can achieve." He told the young people gathered that everything they wanted to accomplish could be theirs. If they would just reach out and grasp it.

"We are belonging to one FAMILY, the human family and the human tribe."

—IZZELDIN ABUELAISH

BARENAKED LADIES
ONE IN A MILLION

With a song about yearning for a million dollars to splurge on fancy ketchup, the elephant man's remains, and tree forts, the Barenaked Ladies have endeared themselves to fans as down-to-earth guys. Literally. The Ladies take their impact on the environment seriously, trying to reduce their carbon footprint by using biofuels in their tour buses, LED lights for their shows, and real cutlery for backstage meals, presumably to eat Kraft Dinner. They rocked the We Day stage singing one of our favorites, "If I Had $1000000." We can think of a lot of worthy ways to spend that amount of money.

"If I had a million dollars I'd buy your LOVE."

—BARENAKED LADIES

MIA FARROW
THE WITNESS

Few celebrities ask to be sent to the most dangerous places on Earth. Actor, mother, and activist Mia Farrow is one of them.

In the immediate aftermath of the devastating Haiti earthquake in 2010, Farrow contacted us to say she'd like to help. But instead of rushing to the scene, she said, "They need emergency workers now, not more celebrities." So a year later, to shine a spotlight on the ongoing needs of the Haitian earthquake victims and visit Free The Children programs, we traveled together to the country's capital, Port-au-Prince. Landing in the midst of post-election violence, poverty, and chaos, we watched as this soft-spoken, petite woman walked into an angry crowd to seek the perspectives of rioters. She photographed burned-out cars and remained steadfast as the mobs pounded on our vehicle.

When the airport closed, TV anchors chartered helicopters to flee the island, but Farrow stayed with us. Together we took the long road, making the 14-hour drive to fly home from the Dominican Republic. Sitting side-by-side, she regaled us with tales about her former husband Frank Sinatra and the infamous Rat Pack, as well as the vats of spaghetti she'd cook up for her 14 children, ten of whom were adopted from difficult circumstances around the world. She also shared with us the roots of her social conscience. A childhood bout with polio that put her in the hospital, and into an iron lung, made her look at the world differently. She was seized by the desire to help others, and for a while dreamed of being a pediatrician in Africa.

She went on to become a celebrated actor, appearing in more than 50 films, including the acclaimed horror movie *Rosemary's Baby*. At 29, her face was on the first-ever cover of *People* magazine. At the time she was known as a Hollywood starlet, who'd hung out with The Beatles at an ashram in India. But today, Farrow, who is a Free The Children Ambassador, is known best for using her fame, compassion, and love of photography to speak out about atrocities in little-publicized conflict zones and to provide hard proof of the plight of displaced peoples.

Her life's work is on behalf of the people of the Darfur region of Sudan, where millions of people have been forced out of their homes to live in wretched camps. She returns again and again to collect their stories, and raise her voice on their behalf.

She told one We Day audience of returning in the aftermath of a helicopter attack, where bombs rained from the skies. The girls—many of them rape victims, who were starving and malnourished—drew pictures of what they had experienced. Using stick figures, one girl sketched a hellish scene of attacking helicopters in the sky, huts on fire, and a Janjaweed militiaman shooting her mother to death. Farrow said she took a picture of the girl's hopeful face and made it the screen saver on her computer. "Whenever I feel dispirited or allow myself to feel a little helpless, I look at her face."

Several months after our adventure with Farrow in Haiti, we visited the Dadaab refugee camp in East Africa. As Farrow met refugees she obliged the hordes of journalists who were following her around with cameras and questions. Later, we returned alone to sit with those same refugees to truly listen to their stories. We met a desperate mother who felt powerless to help her gravely ill child. Farrow took the mother and child to the camp hospital and stayed with them until they got help. There were no cameras to capture this act of kindness.

We are proud to call Farrow our friend and inspiration, especially after the harrowing and thought-provoking journeys we've taken together.

"We are part of a larger human family. When one of us is suffering then all of us are SUFFERING."

—MIA FARROW

ANGÉLIQUE KIDJO
AFRICA'S PREMIER DIVA

One of the most powerful We Day moments was a simple gift. We wanted to thank Archbishop Desmond Tutu for his long-time support and friendship. So we approached Grammy Award–winning singer-songwriter Angélique Kidjo to sing his favorite song to him—live at We Day. And it would be a surprise.

We desperately wanted this to work, but spontaneity does not come easily at an event planned to the minute. *TIME* magazine called Benin-born Kidjo "Africa's premier diva," the most celebrated female singer from that continent. She has an impressive history of giving, in support of girls' education and as a UNICEF Goodwill Ambassador. Still, we weren't sure how this gift would be received. Or if we could pull it off.

After Tutu addressed the audience, the house lights lowered, and Kidjo emerged from the shadows at the back of the arena. Her voice filled the stadium with the entrancing song "Malaika," which is the Swahili word for angel. As she walked toward the stage the Archbishop, stunned and grinning, stood up and began to sway and shuffle. Kidjo climbed the stairs to meet him, and the two danced together.

She didn't miss a beat despite the soaring emotion of the moment. "His spirit is so uplifting, his love and generosity are unstoppable," she said after the show. "I just had to remember to keep singing."

LIGHTS
ON THE ROAD OF LIFE

L ights became a seasoned world traveler long before concert touring had her crisscrossing North America.

The daughter of missionary parents, the Juno Award-winning electro-pop musician and singer (born Valerie Anne Poxleitner) spent her childhood living in the Philippines, Jamaica, and in Eastern and Western Canada. She absorbed cultures and witnessed the world's beauty as well as its hardships—like those in the squatter city of Baseco. Tens of thousands of people live in a square mile of land reclaimed from the Manila Bay that is to this day cramped, disease-ridden, and constantly flooded. "Growing up on the mission field, I was young but I was watching it all," she told us. "I thought, 'How do you change a place like that?' But I came to understand that education is the answer to break people from the cycle of poverty." Lights gives her time to many global causes, including the world of Free The Children.

"You're so impossibly cool for getting up and looking outside of yourselves. Because when you stand for something, there's MOVEMENT where there wasn't movement before."

—LIGHTS

JANE GOODALL
THE PRIMATE PROTECTOR

When Dame Jane Goodall first trekked into the forests of Tanzania in 1960, she had no idea what lay ahead. She couldn't know that her study of chimpanzees would redefine our understanding of the natural world. Or that she would be propelled into international stardom. And she certainly had no idea her work would launch an eminent career as one of the world's most respected conservationists, humanitarians, and animal rights activists. In the very beginning, Goodall was armed only with courage, a passion for animals, and an intense determination to learn.

Nearly four decades later, we had the good fortune to meet Goodall at the 2000 State of the World Forum where we discovered that her intense determination to learn had evolved into a passionate desire to change the world. There were two sessions, a formal congress for world leaders and a separate forum for youth. Goodall crashed the gathering of youth delegates to share her story.

In the 1960s, she defied conventional wisdom that a young woman was not suitable for primatology field research. Backed by the famous paleoanthropologist, Louis Leakey, she ignored these criticisms and immersed herself in a community of chimpanzees to study their social interactions—living in closer proximity to primates than anyone before her. Her observations showed that chimps and humans shared similarities in emotion, behavior, and intelligence. Goodall upended the mainstream belief that the link between the two species was merely genetic.

Her groundbreaking research landed her on the cover of newspapers and magazines the world over. She used her unexpected fame to advocate for the protection of the chimpanzees' natural habitat and become a crusader for animal rights and environmental issues. She founded the Jane Goodall Institute, and started the Roots & Shoots program to inspire young people through community service to preserve the planet for the sake of all living things.

She once told us that she'd succeeded in such an unconventional field because of her mother's wisdom:"Looking back, it's incredible how supportive she was of my admittedly unusual ambitions." She said her mother offered encouragement, "coupled with an intuitive way of knowing how much freedom to grant at a given moment."

At We Day, she thanked her mother, showing that support from a loving parent can make it easier to forge a new path.

"If you really want something, if you really work hard, if you take advantage of OPPORTUNITY, and if you never give up, you will find a way."

—JANE GOODALL

CODY SIMPSON
THE AUSSIE INVASION

When we met Cody Simpson, he was on the heels of his fast track to global fame, with multiple chart-topping hits, coming off of his sold-out Welcome to Paradise Tour. Celebrity hadn't shattered Cody's sense of humility—or any notions that he was still just 15. The entourage waiting backstage for Cody at We Day included Dad, Brad Simpson. Cody still traveled with at least one parental unit.

At the time, he told us about the "great responsibility" he feels as a role model for millions of teens. He connects with fans, in part, through his fearless honesty in the fight against bullying; the issue hits close to home for him and most every teenager. As a public figure, "bullying is something I experience every day online," he said.

At We Day, a bit breathless after his performance, Cody told the crowd about the kids who teased him for pursuing his passion for singing.

"But you know what? I held onto my dream. Everyone should be allowed to follow their dreams. Are you with me, We Day?"

"Everyone should just BELIEVE in themselves. Don't let other people's opinions get in the way."

—CODY SIMPSON

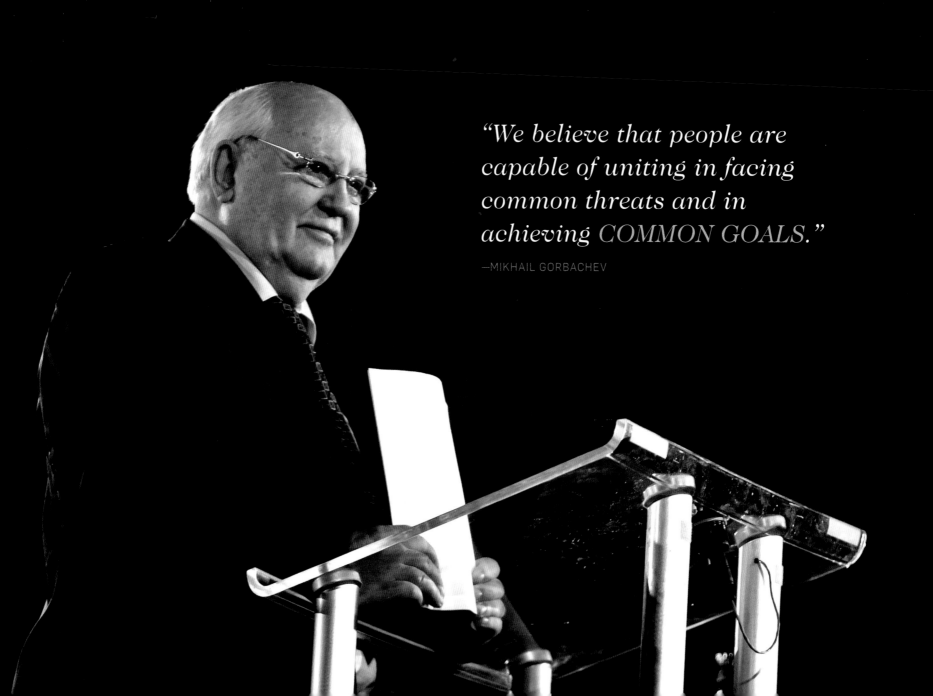

"We believe that people are capable of uniting in facing common threats and in achieving COMMON GOALS."

—MIKHAIL GORBACHEV

MIKHAIL GORBACHEV
THE PEACEMAKER

There's a little chunk of concrete on a shelf in the living room of our parents' home. It's a piece of the Berlin Wall—the once imposing physical divide between East and West Berlin, and the symbol of oppression that stood for decades until its fall in November, 1989.

Back then, our parents called us to see the dramatic events unfold on our small TV set. People celebrated wildly atop the crumbling structure and our parents told us to "remember this moment." We didn't fully understand the significance at the time. But later, having a piece of the wall would be a tangible reminder that anything is possible.

And it would serve as a reminder of the man who made that change happen.

Mikhail Gorbachev paved the way for the fall of the Berlin Wall, the collapse of communism, and the end of the Cold War. At the heart of all his actions was compassion for his fellow human beings.

"Everything I did, I did on the basis of conviction," he told us. "I never acted in revenge. I never acted out of spite. I acted because I felt I wanted to do good."

Despite his motivations, Gorbachev did not exactly enjoy hero status in the United States. While serving as General Secretary of the Communist Party of the Soviet Union from 1985 until 1991, and as the first president of the Soviet Union from 1990 until its dissolution in 1991, he was the enemy.

Even decades later, at We Day events, we noticed that some Americans approached him with trepidation. We thought at first perhaps they were nervous, coming face-to-face with such an iconic figure. But we soon realized that it was because, growing up, Americans were taught to fear this man.

It's fascinating, then, to see him in the proper light—prolific author and Nobel Peace Prize Laureate. He is a loyal and devout family man—his daughter Irina travels everywhere with him—who bucked the system to bring freedom to millions of people.

Gorbachev has been anything but idle since his career as a politician came to an end. His namesake foundation, created in 1991, was built on the belief that we need a new interpretation of progress and humanism to establish a more equitable world order.

His many philanthropic endeavors stem from this want of a better world, but also from personal experience. In 1999, Gorbachev lost his beloved wife, Raisa, following her battle with leukemia. In her honor he co-founded the Raisa Gorbachev Foundation. The nonprofit organization funds lifesaving treatments for young cancer patients and supports research to combat the disease.

Gorbachev is also an environmental advocate who speaks passionately about climate change and the need to preserve the world's natural resources for future generations, including his own five grandchildren.

A conversation with Gorbachev is fascinating. To hear of the many times during the Cold War he was awoken in the middle of the night with threats of a nuclear crisis—any of which might have ended humanity—is downright chilling. You could argue that because Gorbachev held his nerve on those nights, our planet was saved.

Gorbachev's reserve of courage seems limitless. We asked him where it comes from.

"Frankly I do not know. I would not call myself a person of some extraordinary courage." After a long pause, he added: "But I am certainly not a coward."

That's Mikhail Gorbachev, who single-handedly changed the course of history.

"Think about how to live your life in the best possible way. Your thoughts of today will help you in the FUTURE."

—MIKHAIL GORBACHEV

ON THE FUTURE

I have been in politics for 55 years and I can say from experience: never panic, unite, and join your forces and act.

I have faith that your generation will have the strength to cope with the challenges that we are fighting, and to build a society of which we will be proud. A happy society.

Dear friends, future presidents and prime ministers, the future powers to be, do not believe that politics is a dirty business, that it's incompatible with morality. Politics is difficult business. But without a moral core, it is empty, it is just a game of intrigue.

MIKHAIL GORBACHEV, WE DAY 2011

DESMOND TUTU
THE HERO'S HERO

Backstage at We Day is a celeb-spotter's dream come true. From actors and musicians to heads of state and astronauts, there's no shortage of incredible people preparing to inspire a generation to change the world. Then there are some who inspire the inspirers, a select few who elevate everyone with their very presence.

And that's Archbishop Desmond Tutu, who brightens the green room with his infectious laugh or shuffle dance, which surely should be patented.

At We Day, when we ask the celebrities and statesmen about their own heroes, Tutu's name invariably comes up. The Archbishop, meanwhile, tells us his hero is his mother. "I look like her—she had a large nose!—and I often say I wish I would be like her in her compassion and caring of others."

Tutu was South Africa's first black Archbishop. He spoke out against apartheid even though his family was harassed and he was threatened with death. That courage won him the Nobel Peace Prize in 1984. Post-apartheid South Africa was a country full of generations-old anger and hatred. Yet instead of falling into bloodshed, it transitioned peacefully into one of Africa's strongest democracies. Much of that is thanks to the Tutu-led Truth and Reconciliation Commission. He taught a nation, blacks and whites, how to forgive each other and move forward together.

We first met Tutu in Middleburg, the Netherlands, in 1998 when we were recipients of the Roosevelt Freedom Medal, along with the former President of Ireland, Mary Robinson, and American news network CNN.

It was there that he taught us a lesson in gratitude. A line of dignitaries stood by as Tutu's limousine rolled up. The door opened, he emerged and promptly turned his back to everyone. He rapped on the limo's window and when the driver rolled it down, Tutu grabbed his hand and thanked him. Tutu then thanked each member of his police escort and the rest of his entourage before turning his attention to the waiting crowds. How many of us spare a moment to say "thank you" to those who contribute to our lives in all the small ways?

When we were first introduced to Tutu, we stammered out a question: "What do we call you?" He smiled, laid gentle hands on our shoulders, and said, "My friends call me 'the Arch.'" That evening, after receiving his medal, he danced onstage with the African choir.

Later, when Craig was in university, he mentioned to 'the Arch' that he'd stopped reading newspapers. He did not want to start his day facing violence and poverty. "College boy!" Tutu replied. "You are looking at this the wrong way. The newspaper is God's to-do list, delivered to our front door." Staying informed, he said, shifted how he viewed the world and the daily struggles that he could take on. He tells young people, far and wide, that learning about the world informs their passions.

He told us he loves We Day because of the enthusiasm and hope of the young volunteers. "Their idealism is amazing. It just shakes you, to think of the things that they're prepared to do." If he could impart a message to them, it would be "keep on dreaming."

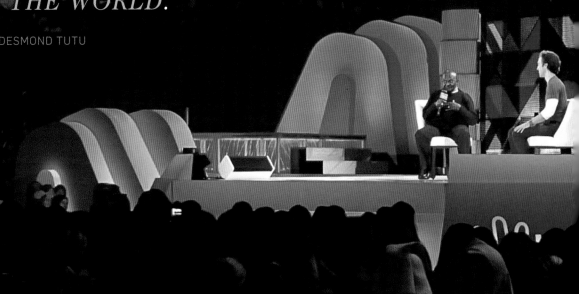

"We would not be free today had it not been for the many people who supported us in the anti-apartheid movement. And many of those were students. Young people. You can CHANGE THE WORLD."

—DESMOND TUTU

THE MOVEMENT OF OUR TIME

EMPOWERING THE GENERATION WE HAVE BEEN WAITING FOR

WE DAY AND WE ACT
INSPIRATION & EMPOWERMENT

Celebrating the power of young people to change the world. That's the promise of We Day.

But each We Day is more than a stadium-sized event; more than the spectacular performers, local heroes, and world-renowned humanitarians onstage who inspire a generation to globalize compassion. We Day is a celebration of young people and their actions through We Act.

We Act is a service learning program that weaves the three Cs into the fold of education: compassion, courage, and community. Through We Act, schools help young people develop the skills they need to succeed academically and in the workplace. The program prepares students to become active local and global citizens by instilling the values of critical thinking, knowledge about social issues, and an understanding about the impact of every individual's actions and choices on the world around them. The program also empowers young people to take tangible actions that make a difference on the issues they care about. Youth can't buy a ticket to We Day—they earn it through service.

With We Act, schools and youth groups commit to take at least one local and one global action. In return, they receive mentor support, educational tools, resources, and action campaigns to make their We Act commitments come to life.

The ripple effect of their service is felt in their communities and around the world. We Act schools have stocked the shelves of local food banks with millions of pounds of food. These same students are linked to sister schools overseas through Adopt a Village, a holistic program that removes barriers to education by building schools and providing clean water, health care, and sustainable sources of food and income. For years to come, We Act youth and alumni are more likely than their peers to volunteer, give to charity, and vote in federal elections.

More than an event, We Day celebrates the movement of young people leading change through We Act.

"Perhaps the biggest impact was that students now feel like part of a bigger community that is concerned about social and environmental issues. They are more MOTIVATED AND EMPOWERED to take on leadership roles."

—CONSTANZA GARDEAZABAL AND FRANK DELORENZIS, EDUCATORS

WE ACT RESOURCES
PREPARING STUDENTS TO BE ACTIVE CITIZENS

We Act program resources help educators bring social issues and service learning into the classroom. Open to all schools, the core program and resources are available to schools at no cost. The enhanced program components are available in certain regions through the support of sponsors.

CORE RESOURCES

Support staff
A team of full-time Youth Programming Coordinators that mentor and help educators and students to plan and fulfill their service commitment.

Educational materials
Built as issues-based modules, our library of online lesson plans can be easily implemented into classrooms, after-school programs, and family learning. Educators also receive weekly e-mailed lesson plans on current events.

Service campaigns
Delivered online or as a printed kit, our campaigns and other pre-packaged resources address local and global issues, such as homelessness, hunger, children's rights, clean water, and more.

Fundraising tool kits
Specially designed kits include wall-sized posters for each Adopt a Village pillar. The kits help youth set goals and track their fundraising in support of development projects in Asia, Africa, or Latin America.

Online community
Our social networks connect youth and educators with the issues they care about and the actions they want to take.

ENHANCED RESOURCES

Speaking tours
Youth speakers deliver motivational speeches on relevant topics to entire student bodies, followed by workshops with a smaller group of student leaders to help them identify their passions and create action plans.

Youth summits
In a series of workshops, these one-day summits bring young people together to learn about the root causes of social problems as they develop leadership skills and action plans to tackle local and global challenges.

Professional development for educators
Educator workshops offer effective models for teaching and engaging students on social issues; ideas for differentiated instruction; and networking opportunities to enhance both extracurricular and classroom-based engagement.

International volunteer trips
Youth and school groups are invited to visit the Adopt a Village community in Africa, Asia, or Latin America they have supported through their fundraising efforts. Each Me to We trip opens a world of learning and adventure as young people volunteer alongside local community members to build a school, become immersed in local culture, and gain a different perspective of the world.

217

CAMPAIGNS KIT
SNAPSHOT OF ACTION CAMPAIGNS

We Act empowers young people to take action on any cause or issue they care about. But, their teachers are provided with pre-packaged campaign kits and resources to help them get started. Kits can be ordered online at no cost. Here are snapshots of just a few.

We Scare Hunger

Millions of people in our communities go hungry every day. Each fall, young people trick-or-treat at Halloween for non-perishable food items or collect canned goods at school and in their communities for Thanksgiving food drives to support their local food banks.

We are Silent

For the millions of children around the world who are silenced by the denial of their basic human rights, young people take a vow of silence for 24 hours. They don't speak, but they tweet, post, and share their experience while raising awareness about why they are silent. They also collect pledges for every hour of silence to help children and their families overseas break the cycle of poverty.

We Create Change

Young people collect small change to make a big impact. This coin drive focuses on a different denomination every year in support of a specific cause. In the 2012-2013 academic year, youth collected more than 130 million pennies, with every $25 providing one person with clean drinking water for life.

Adopt a Village

Free The Children's holistic and sustainable development model, Adopt a Village is designed to meet the basic needs of developing communities and eliminate the obstacles preventing children from accessing education. Through Adopt a Village, young people connect with specific communities, support development projects, learn about the region, raise awareness, and even travel overseas to visit the communities and volunteer alongside the local people.

"The program has impacted our school in many ways. The student leaders have literally FLOURISHED before my eyes. They are mature, confident, responsible, and creative young people."

—LAURA DE SIMONE, EDUCATOR

WE SCARE HUNGER
Community Food Drive
Wednesday October 31
440 food items!

WE ARE THE MOB
WE ARE THE MASSES
WE ARE THE MOVEMENT

WE CREATE CHANGE

ADOPT A VILLAGE CLEAN WATER PROGRAM

CHARITY CAR WASH!

START FUNDRAISING NOW!

DIGITAL PLATFORM
WE365: SOCIAL GOOD THROUGH SOCIAL ACTION

Want to change the world, every day? It's in your hands! No, literally, we put the power to change the world right in your hands.

We365 is a mobile app that empowers youth to create a portfolio of their social impact, while connecting with friends and classmates to create a community that is centered on actions for social good. It is a tool to track and verify volunteer hours for school, scholarships, and resumes.

And that's just the beginning. Download the We365 app and be a part of daily challenges to make the world a better place. Care about endangered species? There's a challenge for that. Passionate about putting an end to bullying? We've got a challenge for that, too. Discover your cause on We365 and take action to impact your community and our planet. We365 is an initiative of Free The Children and Telus.

With the We365 app you can:

- Join a community of people who care

- Take daily challenges for social good

- Track and verify your volunteer hours

- Build a social impact portfolio to help support school, internship and scholarship applications

And most importantly, remember: you can make a difference every day… and have fun while you're at it!

A STORY IN NUMBERS

THE IMPACT OF WE DAY & WE ACT

$32M RAISED
FOR MORE THAN **1,000 LOCAL AND GLOBAL CAUSES**

6M HRS
VOLUNTEERED FOR LOCAL AND GLOBAL CAUSES

2M
YOUNG PEOPLE FROM AROUND THE WORLD
TAKE PART IN PROGRAMS AND CAMPAIGNS

4M LBS
OF **FOOD COLLECTED** FOR LOCAL FOOD BANKS

160,000
STUDENTS FROM 4,000 SCHOOLS
PARTICIPATE ANNUALLY IN WE DAY EVENTS

97%
OF STUDENTS **BELIEVE THEY CAN MAKE A DIFFERENCE** AFTER ATTENDING WE DAY

85%
OF EDUCATORS FIND A GREATER **ATMOSPHERE OF CARING AND COMPASSION** IN THE SCHOOL

82%
OF STUDENTS HAVE DEMONSTRATED **INCREASED LEADERSHIP** AMONG THEIR PEERS

80%
OF WE ACT ALUMNI **VOLUNTEER MORE THAN 150 HOURS EACH YEAR**

83%
OF ALUMNI **MADE A FINANCIAL CONTRIBUTION TO A NONPROFIT** OR CHARITY IN THE LAST YEAR

79%
OF WE ACT ALUMNI 18-YEARS OR OLDER **VOTED IN THE PREVIOUS NATIONAL ELECTION**

Based on an independent impact assessment report prepared by Mission Measurement, LLC

they say to understand
someone
you have to
walk a mile in their shoes

A STORY IN WORDS
THE IMPACT OF WE DAY & WE ACT

"Our intermediates this year have been incredible. One student who had attendance issues started COMING TO SCHOOL MORE because she had a purpose."

—ANTIONETTE PAYNE, EDUCATOR

"Students who would normally walk by bullying or vandalism or some other action that degrades our school community are more likely to STAND UP AND SAY SOMETHING."

—KERRI-ANN MACKAY, EDUCATOR

"Parents are PROUD OF THEIR CHILDREN for demonstrating knowledge and compassion for others."

—TARA FISHER, EDUCATOR

"Our school climate has changed dramatically. Bullying was an issue in our school before. Different people, from parents to administrators, always say they can FEEL A DIFFERENCE now when they walk into our school. It is a much more caring community!"

—LAURA MUZZELL, EDUCATOR

MAKENZIE JESSE
THE GO-GETTER

Pedaling 100 kilometers in 100 days. Makenzie Jesse set this goal to fundraise and contribute to her school's goal of building a well in Kenya. For many, this may not seem ambitious. But for the 13 year old, it was a daily distance—just short of a mile—that would test her endurance. She has cerebral palsy, which affects movement in her lower body.

Makenzie was inspired by the story of Spencer West (pg.38) who, having lost both legs at the age of five, went on to climb Mount Kilimanjaro on his hands and in his wheelchair to raise funds for a cause he believed in. Spencer called his campaign "Redefine Possible," and Makenzie was determined to do the same.

On Day 1, it took Makenzie about 20 minutes to pedal the kilometer. Over many days, she cut that time in half. And on the final day, pedaling to the cheers of "go, Makenzie, go" from more than 500 of her schoolmates, teachers and family, she reached her goal in five minutes. Already a hero to her community, Makenzie also raised more than $5,000 over the 100 days.

"Makenzie has a beautiful SPIRIT *and always stops to help those in need. I learn from Makenzie every day."*

—SHALAIN, MAKENZIE'S MOM

226

CALEB DAWSON
THE MOBILISER

In the seventh grade, Caleb Dawson knew "little" about himself and "even less about how to help others." But he knew he had a passion to make a difference. He and his family were missionaries, so he knew about the stark realities of poverty. He knew there were parts of the world where children lived in cardboard shacks and used the local dump as a playground.

With the help of his teacher, Mr. Joe Hunich, Caleb also came to learn about how hunger and homelessness affected his own community. That year, Mr. Hunich planted a seed in Caleb's mind about a Halloween food drive.

The seed blossomed in the tenth grade, when Caleb rallied friends to collect canned food. By senior year, Caleb and his friends mobilized more than 350 students across school districts. They invested thousands of volunteer hours to organize 253 "We Scare Hunger" food drives. Together, they collected more than 12,500 pounds of food. Their contribution benefited 3,140 individuals—the largest ever donation of food to the Multi-Service Center in Caleb's community.

"It's never too late to get started. We are the answer to our world's crisis. WE ARE THE CHANGE!"

—CALEB DAWSON

ABBIE LUMANI
THE RUNNER

During a three-week volunteer trip to the dusty plains of Kenya's Maasai Mara, Abbie Lumani walked in another's footsteps. Led by Mama Purity and Mama Rose, Abbie and 31 other young volunteers made a three-mile trek to fetch water from the nearest source. They each filled their 5.3-gallon jerry cans with the brown, muddied water and then walked back the same distance. Maasai mamas and their daughters cheered Abbie's return, all grateful the volunteers had carried their water on that particular day.

Abbie thought about how, at home, cold, clean water came from a tap, usually only a few steps away. Anything extra was thrown down a sink. It was both perspective and a spark.

Abbie came home with the goal of fundraising at least $5,000 through her initiative, Picture This—Quenching Kenya's Thirst, by holding a run. With the support of more than 200 runners, she doubled her goal, raising $10,000 for clean water projects for an entire community in rural Kenya.

"After my trip, I treat water much differently. My EXPERIENCE made me reflect on a lot of things."

—ABBIE LUMANI

MARK MANNARN
THE HOCKEY HERO

After an inspiring We Day, 12-year-old Mark Mannarn had an idea: combine something he loved—hockey—with something he hated—cancer.

Mark's Oma (German for grandmother) had recently been diagnosed with terminal pancreatic cancer. In her last days, Mark visited his Oma every day. He didn't think it could get any worse. But then his mom was diagnosed with breast cancer. Mark was scared he would lose her, too.

To deal with the anguish of his Oma's worsening condition and his mom's pending double lumpectomy, Mark set a goal to raise $100,000 to fight cancer.

With his dad's encouragement, Mark came up with Minor Hockey Fights Cancer to empower kids to raise money for cancer and give them the chance to play hockey with NHL stars.

For months, Mark busily organized his charity event, reached out to NHL greats, met with sponsors, pitched his plan to other kids, and wrote letters to the NHL Alumni Association and every NHL team to donate jerseys, pucks, and sticks for the silent auction.

On event day, Mark played with hockey legends—one of the most meaningful hour of his life. And not because Hockey Hall of Famer Paul Coffey passed him the puck or because his team won. He had doubled his goal, raising more than $200,000. And he's not finished yet. His 'Feel Like a Pro Day' has now become an annual event.

"What I like about hockey is that it's a team sport and you can't win without a good TEAM. *I had an amazing group of volunteers organizing an event that was quickly approaching. I couldn't believe how many people came forward to help."*

—MARK MANNARN

WE DAY CHAMPIONS
WITH A LITTLE HELP FROM OUR FRIENDS

It takes a village to empower a generation of youth. We give our heartfelt gratitude to a community of friends and supporters who have been among our greatest champions in every endeavor.

Kannan Aarasaratnam
A Better Seattle
Lori Adams
Mark Addicks
David Aisenstat
Michael Akkawi
Alberta Education
Ron Alepian
Paul Allen
Allstate Corporation
Amanda Alvaro
Amway
Shane Ankeney
Susan Antonacci
Francesco Aquilini
Tali'ah Aquilini and family
Ariad Communications
Lisa Arnold
Gail Asper
National Chief Shawn Atleo
Jonathan Atwood
Shari Austin

Marie-Anne Aymerich
Sharon Babineau
Akhtar Badshah
Jim Baller
Connie and Steve Ballmer
Jordan Banks
Barclays
Deb and Steve Barnes
Geneviève Barrière
Richard Bartrem
Dany Battat
Joseph Battat
David Baum
Richard Beaven
Mike Bechtol
Scott and Cheri Beck and family
Michael Beckerman
Wanda Bedard
The Beecham Family
Theresa Beenken
Jan Belanger
Pascale Belanger

Bell Media
Kevin Bent
Jim Berk
Chris Besse
The Bezos Family
Brian Bidulka
Big Change Charitable Trust
The Bigue-Tuli Foundation
Bill and Melinda Gates Foundation
Andrew Black and family
Willa Black
Blackberry
Josh Blair
Rob Blanchard
David Bley
David Boardman
Boardwalk Rental Communities
Bogani Family Coalition
Natasha Borota
Brian Bost
Gina Boswell
Susanne Boyce

Jeff Boyd
Rick Brace
Jill Brady
Marylou Brannan
Holly Branson
Sir Richard Branson
Bremer Bank
Otto Bremer Foundation
Nicola Brentnall
Heather Briant
Jenny Brigden
British Columbia Ministry of Education
Jane Broom
Hon. Laurel C. Broten
Barbara Brotherson
Sheryl Brown
Andy Bryant
Anna Bryce
Budhdeo Family Foundation
Mindy Budhdeo
Naman Budhdeo

Suzana Bulhoes

Craig Burkinshaw and
Joanne Le Bon

Suzanne Burrows

Brendan and Sandra Caldwell
and family

Calgary Flames Hockey Club

Gordon and Nancy Campbell

Canad Inns

Canadian Living

Capilano University

Carlson Family Foundation

Marilyn Carlson Nelson

Chris and Tania Carnegie

Coach Pete and Glena Carroll

Susan Cayne

Rob Chad

The Chainani Family

Lynn Chambers

Cheerios

Mark Chipman

Wayne Chiu

Iain Christiansen

Jeff and Linda Church and family

Cineplex Entertainment

Ian Clarke

Clear Channel

Michael and Diane Clemons
and family

Dame Julia Cleverdon

The Clunie Family

CPA Alberta

David Cohen

Josh Cohen

Stephanie Cohen

Sue Coliton

David Conklin

Gerry Connelly

Taylor Conroy

Kim Cooper

Matthew Corrin

Lynne Corvaglia

Reed Cowan

Bob Cox

Dianne Craig

Jeanne Crain

Kelly Creeden

Janet Crown and Steve Robinson

John Cruickshank

Kevin Crull

CTV and MuchMusic

Rob Cummings

John Danakas

Kimberly Dasher-Tripp

Heidi Davidson

Beverly Deikel

Jason Dehni

Drew Descourouez

Virginia Devlin

Victoria Dinges

DHL Express Canada

Joe Diubaldo

Phil Donne

Kevin Donnelly

Mary-Eileen Donovan

Pat Donovan

Michelle Douglas

William Doyle

Tonya Dressel

Francine Dyksterhuis

Edel Ebbs

Education First

The Edward J. Phillips Family
Foundation

Charlotte Empey

ENMAX

Darren Entwistle

Hamid Eshgi

Sid Espinosa

Kevin Espirito

Carolyn and Doug Everson
and family

Brian Felesky

David and Karen Feltch and family

Sarah Fenton

Jonathon Fischer

Connie Fontaine

Ford

Scott Ford

Sian Foster

Freshii

Rick Frost

Paul Furia

Nelly Furtado

Ian Gadsby

Dr. John and Dorthea Gaither

Bill and Mimi Gates and family

General Mills

Ginny Gilder

Michael Girgis

Tasha Giroux

Stuart Gold

Don Gonsalves

Lucas Goodenough

Charlotte Goodman

The Ghorbani Family

John Gordon

Tom Gosner

Craig Gosselin

John Graham

Patricia Graham

Shane Grant

Trudy Grant

Jim Gray

Green Giant

Drew Green

Jason Green

Walter Green

Tom Greenberg

Kevin Griffin

Sanjay Gupta

Alden Hadwen

Stanley Hainsworth

Halifax Regional Municipality

Eva and Dr. Yoel Haller

The Hanauer Family

Lori Harnick

Jori Hartwig

Lord Michael Hastings

Jayne Haugen Olson

Tony Hauser

Hedley

Craig and Libby Heimark and family

Thorsten Heins

The Henry Family

Greg Hewitt

The Hickey Family

Ella Hohnen-Ford

Holt Renfrew

Cathy Honor

Heidi Hopper and Jeff Dean and family

Adrian Horwood

The Housenbold Family

Stephen Huddart

Susan Hughes

Eddie Hult

Guy Huntingford

Investors Group

Richard Irish

Jeff Ivers

Ellis Jacob

James Richardson & Sons Limited

Antony and Amanda Jenkins

Hamish Jenkinson

The John D. Brule family

Charlotte Johnson

Eric and Shannon Johnson

Rob Johnston

His Excellency the Rt. Hon. David Johnston, Governor General of Canada

Chris Jones

Amanda Jordan

Singfield Joyle

Brian Kalliecharan

Anita Kaushal

John Kearsey

Jacki and Jack Kelley and family

Maryann Kempe

Gavin Kennedy and family

Tenille Kennedy

Brien Kennedy

Cynthia Kersey

Nicola Kettlitz

Ken King

Phil King

Dr. Ann and Robert Klamar

Tom Kloet

Lee Knafelc

Sean Knierem

Wendy and Jeff Kohn

Sam Kolias

KPMG LLP

Keith Krach

Dan Kranzler

Craig Kreeger

Dave Krysko and family

Chris Krywulak

Lynda, Stan, and Mitch Kurylowicz

Leonard Kurz

Wendy Lachance

George E. Lafond

Guy Laliberté

Pauline Latham

Jeffrey Latimer

Leo Ledehowski

Harry Leibowitz

Randy Lennow

Dan'l Lewin

Mary Lewis

Don Lindsay

Brian Lipschultz

Lili Liu

Anthony Longo

Demi Lovato

Lisa Love

Ellen Goldberg Luger

Amy Lui

Thomas Lundgren

Bruce Mackenzie

Natasha Mackow

Graham MacLachlan

Oliver Madison

Ben Malcolmson

The Mallet Family

Rene Malo

Peter McLoughlin

Manitoba Ministry of Education

The Maritz Family

Allan and Patricia Markin

Cliff Marks and family

Martin Aboriginal Education Initiative

David Martin

Kimi Martin

Rt. Hon. Paul Martin

Kim Mason

Kim Mathewes

Candace Matthews

Jane McCaig

Karla McCormick

Grant McDonald

David McKay

Rob McLaughlin

Della and Stuart McLaughlin

Donna McNicol

The McPhedran family

Peter Mears

Mediabrands

Lane and Maegan Merrifield

The Merrifield Family

Margot Micallef

Microsoft

Brad and Marion Miller

David and Jennifer Miller

Minnesota Department of Education

Minnetonka Moccasin

Kara Mitchelmore

Tammy Mok

Leslie Molin

Doug Moore

Minister James Moore

Sarah Moote

Cheri Moreau

Don and Debbie Morrison

Dr. Djavid Mowafaghian

Stacey Mowbray

Graham Moysey
MTS Sports and Entertainment
Patrick Mullins
Harold Munro
Bob Murphy
Lynee Nailer
The Narayen Family
David Nelson
Kim Nelson
Nelson Education
Michael Nobrega
Greg Nordal
Nordstrom
Erik Nordstrom
The Norvig Family
Gerry Nott
Government of Nova Scotia, Education and Early Childhood Development
Darci Nyal
The Oakland Athletics
The Oakland Raiders
Sheila O'Gorman
Jean Olewang
OMERS Worldwide
Ontario Ministry of Education
Sally Osberg
Tina Osen
Our Generation
Hannah Owen
Stephanie Pace Marshall
PacSun

Pareto
Participant Media
Pattison OneStop
Pam Pearson
Sylvie Pelletier
Mary Pembroke Perlin
Dean Phillips and family
Hutton Phillips
Jay Phillips
Tyler Phillips
Jamie Pitblado
Natalie Portman
PotashCorp
The Priebe Family
Geraldine Prosser
The Prosser Family
Q13 FOX News
Queens Silver Jubilee Trust
Sanam Quraishi
Karen Radford
Jeffrey and Tricia Raikes
Haroon Rashid
RBC
Daniel Reardon
Jennifer Redmond
Jeff Reed
Doug Reid
Heather Reisman
Jennifer Reynolds
Corinne Richardson
Hartley Richardson
Sue Riddell Rose

The Rittweger Family
Paul Roer
Greg Rogers
Ernan Roman
Linda Rosier
Bruce and Lisa Rothney and family
Richard Rousseau
Sylvie Roy
Royal Ottawa Golf Club
The Rumi Foundation
Nicole Rustad
Ken Ryals
Sabey Corporation
Dave Sabey
Joe Sabey
Mauricio Sabogal
John and Nancy Sabol and family
Michael Samosewzki
Paul Samyn
Dave Goldberg and Sheryl Sandberg
Department of Children, Youth and Their Families, San Francisco
The San Francisco Giants
The San Jose Sharks Foundation
Lucie Santoro
Gregg Saretsky
Lily Kanter and Marc Sarosi
Jason Saul
Mayor Mike Savage
Jos and Tanya Schmitt
Jill Schnarr

Gary Schoenfeld
Janice Schoening
Linda Schuyler
Hal Schwartz
Kevin Screpnechuk
Seattle Storm
Kathryn Seargent
Seattle Seahawks
Barry Segal
Joseph Segal
Lorne and Melita Segal and family
Matt and Russlyn Seiler and family
David Sersta
Kerry and Mandy Shapansky
Glenn Sheen
Tricia Silliphant
Bob Silver
Dick Simon
Neil Skelding
Jeff Skoll
Gary Slaight
Brad Smith
David and Britt Solo and family
Kira Sorensen
Rhonda Speiss
Tim Spencer
Juliana Sprott
John Stackhouse
Denita Stann
Andy and Cass Stillman
Michael and Karen Stone and family
Subway (Alberta)

Kevin Sullivan
Bruny Surin
Gregg Swedberg
The Swidler Family
Angela Taggart
Julie Taggart
Michael Tait
Murray Taylor
Neil Taylor
Team London
Katie Telford
TELUS
Tether
The Allstate Foundation
The Beverly Foundation
The Edward J. Phillips
Family Foundation

The Keg Steakhouse & Bar/
The Keg Spirit Foundation
The Paul G. Allen Family Foundation
The Second Cup Ltd.
The Skoll Foundation
Martin Thibodeau
Bill Thomas
Yvonne Thomas
Margaret Thomson
Carolyn Torhjelm
Jennifer Tory
John Tory and family
Denis Trottier
Greg Twinney
Unilever
Louis Vachon
Danielle Valiquette

Stacey Van Horn
Kevin Van
Rumi Verjee
Micheline Villeneuve
Les Viner
Bill and Lisa Vipond
Jillian Vitale
Tanios Viviani and family
Gisela Voss and family
Brooke and Tracey Wade and family
Veronica Wadley
Bruno Wall
Alex Walters
WCCO
Phyllis Weiner
Ryan Weldon
WestJet

Alexandra Weston
Michelle Weswaldi
Cathy Whelan Molloy
David Wheldon
Dr. Jonathan White
Shelley White
Thomas J. Wilson
Heather Wingate
Lori Yarchuck
Yoplait
Jeffrey York and family
Dr. Alison Young
YPO/WPO/EO
Zinc & Heath/ Teck Resources LTD.

THE POWER OF WE
THANKS TO OUR CREATIVE TEAM

Writing this book was an act of "we"—a collective effort, with support, words, and wisdom from an incredible team.

This book would not have been possible without the tremendous efforts of Executive Editor Shelley Page and Production Manager Katie Hewitt. We cannot sufficiently express our gratitude to Shelley for her leadership, patience, and the creative vision that helped hold our project, and our team, together. Katie, a contrarian by nature with a surprising amount of information about teen idols and popular culture, brought to this project her good humor, impressive organizational skills, and a critical eye. Thanks to you both for helping put our stories into words.

A special thank you to designer Erin Aubrey for taking creative risks, and for jumping wholeheartedly into this ambitious project. Thanks to Kieran Green for his commitment to quality and Sean Deasy for explaining the difference between "stand alone" and "pull out" quotes and for touring with We Day to gather stories, among his many contributions. We are indebted to Michael Pitblado for his research skills, attention to pedantic detail, and reserve of sports history knowledge.

With the care and creativity that she brings to all of her work, Sapna Goel built a beautiful book-within-a-book to showcase some of the amazing young people, teachers, and We Day supporters. Ryan Bolton, a veteran of our many book projects, brought his wealth of experience to the process. We are grateful to Frances Data for drafting the initial layout options.

Finally, thanks to Vito Amati, Scott Ramsay, and Michael Rajzman for many of the stellar images that help make up We Day's visual history.

241

ON THE FRONTLINES
THANKS TO THE WE DAY TEAM

We like to say that it takes a village to raise We Day. And we are forever grateful to the countless people who pull off this minor miracle in 13 cities (and counting) around the world each year. Many leave their hometowns, families, significant others, pets, and personal lives to join the We Day tour—to be on the frontlines of the We movement.

We want to offer our immense gratitude and sincere thanks to the incredible We Day team in Canada, the United States, and the United Kingdom for bringing this movement together and for taking it global. From producing the shows, securing top talent, engaging honored guests, acquiring business development partnerships, fulfilling sponsorship needs, working on event operations and logistics, and garnering publicity, your hard work and dedication make it possible. Thank you for living We Day every day.

On show days, the success of these teams is shared and supported by our amazing Free The Children and Me to We staff, as well as volunteers, who transform stadiums with impeccable precision as part of the following teams: decor, booths, digital media, special events and experiences, inputs, load in/out, volunteer coordination, seating, catering, tech, transportation and safety, venue relations, crowd-pumping, wrangling, and of course, human power—a team designed to tackle the odd jobs that no one anticipated.

Every show is an adventure, and we could never do it without you. Thank you.

PHOTOGRAPHS
A THOUSAND WORDS

The following photographers captured We Day moments and generously shared their images for use in this book.

Sarah Alston
Vito Amati
Artbound
Roger Aziz
Richard Beaven
Bell Media
Adam Bettcher
Nicole Marie Bienvenu
Alec Bozzo
Matthew Broszkowski
Chris Cameron
Sara Cornthwaite
Josee Caza
Carmen Cheung
Michael Collopy
John Delaney
Jen Dibble
Eric Dreger

Dwarka
Vanessa Fukuyama
Lyndsay Greenwood
V. Tony Hauser
Becka Heck
Bryan Heck
Heydemann Art of Photography
Ross Howey
Erika Jacobs
Jeff Jewiss
Peter Kisil
Keri Knapp
Jason Kwan
Mark Luciani
Jamie Macdonald
Wayne Mah
Lesley Marino
Greg Masuda

Christine McAvoy
Christina McWilliams
Dave Meisner
Ryan Miller
Steve Miller
Phil Ogynist
Barry Panas
Julie Pasila
Greg Paupst
Jon Peters
Jasmin Poon
Candice Popik
Michael Rajzman
Scott Ramsay
Erin Riley
Chelsea Roisum
Della Rollins
Josh Sam

Francine Scott
Vanessa Shakespeare
Sai Sivanesan
R. Skelly
Tracy Southey
Manuela Stefan
Tatiana St-Pierre
Sunny Szpak-Holly
Jonathan Taggart
David Thai
Twitchy Finger Photography
James Vander Woerd
Andrew Ventura
Angela Wiens
Robin Wong
Shannon Wong

STAY CONNECTED WITH THE MOVEMENT

LEARN MORE ABOUT FREE THE CHILDREN & ME TO WE

FREE THE CHILDREN
WE ARE THE CHANGE

Free The Children is an international charity and educational partner. Domestically through We Day and We Act, we educate, engage and empower youth to become active citizens. Internationally, our sustainable development model, Adopt a Village, removes barriers to education and empowers communities to break the cycle of poverty.

Get involved with Free The Children:

- Donate. $25 gives one person clean water for life; $8,500 builds a classroom.

- Support one of our five development pillars such as building a school or water project for a village. Use our tracking tools to keep engagement high and the goal in sight.

- Adopt an entire village. Bring your school, family, company or group together to fundraise for all five pillars, and help transform a whole community.

Visit **www.freethechildren.com** to find out more.

ME TO WE
WE LIVE THE CHANGE

Me to We is an innovative social enterprise that provides people with better choices for a better world, and measures the bottom line by the number of lives we change. Half of Me to We's net profit is donated to Free The Children and the other half is reinvested to grow the enterprise.

Embrace Me to We:

- Experience life-changing volunteer trips around the world.

- Wear Me to We Artisans, accessories with a purpose.

- Sport Me to We Style, domestically produced, sweatshop-free clothing.

- Exercise choice with socially conscious and environmentally friendly products.

Visit **www.metowe.com** to find out more.

ME TO WE
VOLUNTEER TRAVEL & SPEAKERS BUREAU

TAKE A LIFE-CHANGING VOLUNTEER TRIP

Interested in a volunteer travel experience that changes your perspective, while positively transforming the lives of others?

On a Me to We Trip, you will help build schools, teach children, and discover age-old cultures. The experience provides a deeper sense of gratitude about life's simple blessings.

Our staff welcome you into the communities where they live and work. In complete safety and comfort, more than 3,000 adventurous people of all ages have chosen to volunteer abroad with us. We welcome youth, families, companies, and groups.

Visit **www.metowe.com/trips** to learn more.

GET INSPIRED BY OUR SPEAKERS

Bring a speaker to your child's school, your workplace, or conferences—and take away all you need to "be the change."

Me to We Speakers offers the most inspirational people with remarkable life experiences. You've read some of their amazing stories—like that of Spencer West (pg.38), Robin Wiszowaty (pg.186), and Molly Burke (pg.54)—now invite them to share more. From community activists to social entrepreneurs, our roster of energetic, experienced speakers are leading the Me to We movement: living and working in developing communities, helping businesses achieve social responsibility, and inspiring auditoriums of youth and educators to action.

They'll make you laugh, cry, and gain a new perspective on what really matters. Be warned: their passion is contagious!

Visit **www.metowe.com/speakers** to learn more.

BOOKS
WITH A REAL MESSAGE

Me to We
Craig and Marc Kielburger
Me to We is a manual, a manifesto, and a movement. It's about finding meaning in our lives and our world by reaching out to others. In this book, Craig and Marc Kielburger share their knowledge, complimented and reinforced by contributors like Richard Gere, Dr. Jane Goodall, Her Majesty Queen Noor, and Oprah Winfrey.

Free the Children
Craig Kielburger
This is the story that launched a movement. *Free the Children* recounts 12-year-old Craig Kielburger's remarkable odyssey across South Asia, meeting some of the world's most disadvantaged children, exploring slums and sweatshops and fighting to rescue children from the chains of inhumane conditions.

My Grandma Follows Me on Twitter: And Other First World Problems We're Lucky to Have
Craig and Marc Kielburger
My Grandma Follows Me On Twitter is a side-splitting collection of first world problems with real world solutions guaranteed to give pause for both gratitude and laughter.

My Maasai Life
Robin Wiszowaty
In her early 20s, Robin Wiszowaty left the ordinary world behind to join a traditional Maasai family. With full-color photographs from her adventures, Robin's heart-wrenching story will inspire you to question your own definitions of home, happiness, and family.

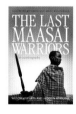

The Last Maasai Warriors
Wilson Meikuaya and Jackson Ntirkana
Wilson and Jackson are brave warriors of the Maasai, an intensely proud culture built on countless generations steeped in the mystique of tradition, legend, and prophecy. They represent the final generation to literally fight for their way of life—they are the last of the great warriors.

Standing Tall
Spencer West
Navigating life on his hands, Spencer had always lived with purpose. This is the candid, coming-of-age story of a young man's journey of working hard, laughing a lot and always standing tall.

The World Needs Your Kid
Craig and Marc Kielburger and Shelley Page
This unique guide to parenting advances the philosophy of the three C's: compassion, courage, and community, which encourage children to become global citizens. The book draws on life lessons from remarkable individuals like Elie Wiesel and Archbishop Desmond Tutu.

Living Me to We
Craig and Marc Kielburger
We all want to make a difference. Now it's easier to lead a life that makes the world a better place every day. With this specifically Canadian guide, readers are provided tips from morning to bedtime. Contributions from your favorite Canadians, such as Margaret Atwood and Rick Hanson.

Global Voices, The Compilation: Vol. 1
Craig and Marc Kielburger
Global Voices aims to tell the untold stories of people and issues from around the world. This book will inspire young readers to deepen their understanding of issues and explore how they can change these headlines.

BOOKS
FOR YOUNGER READERS

Everyone's Birthday
Marc Kielburger

A birthday celebration in Thailand changes the course of a young Marc Kielburger's life. With full-color illustrations, follow Marc in this true story about discovering the importance of celebrating life's many blessings.

Lessons From a Street Kid
Craig Kielburger

It was on the streets of Brazil that Craig learned first-hand a lesson in generosity from the street children. This full-color illustrated children's book teaches that we all have gifts to share.

My Maasai Life: A Child's Adventure in Kenya
Robin Wiszowaty

Follow a young Robin Wiszowaty on the adventure of a lifetime, living among Maasai on her first visit to Kenya. In this true story, crafted for children and with full-color illustrations, Robin explores the land and culture of the Maasai Mara—a place she would one day call home.

Visit **www.metowe.com/books** to see our full list of bestselling books.

The Buy a Book, Give a Book promise ensures that for every Me to We book purchased, a notebook will be given to a child in a developing country.

STAY CONNECTED WITH THE WE DAY MOVEMENT

 we365.com   twitter.com/craigkielburger   facebook.com/weday

Go to **www.weday.com** to see a We Day in a city near you.